Ho L..... Your First Job & Make A Success Of It

By Ramon Greenwood

You can get the job you really want and make it work for you.

Common Sense At Work©

Copyright©

COMMON SENSE PUBLISHING COMPANY
P.O. Box 1581
Pine Bluff, Arkansas 71613
Telephone (501) 536-5468
Fax (501) 536-3344

HOW TO LAND YOUR FIRST JOB
&
MAKE A SUCCESS OF IT

ISBN 0-9642123-0-7

Library of Congress Card Catalogue Number 94-72325

First published in the United States of America in 1994 by Common Sense Publishing Company.

This book is dedicated to our five granddaughters:
Emily and Katherine Riemer;
Lauren, Joanna and Melissa Greenwood.
They have made our lives richer in every way.

A QUESTION YOU SHOULD ASK

You should satisfy yourself on a crucial question before you invest your time in reading this book and relying on it in your job search.

Who is Ramon Greenwood and why is he qualified to provide advice on how to land your first job and make a success of it?

First of all, his advice is based on a rich lode of experience gained during a long and varied career as a corporate executive; a management consultant; an entrepreneur; a government official; and a writer.

He has served as a senior vice president of American Express Company, and a senior public affairs officer in President Gerald Ford's Administration. He has been a senior executive in two other *Fortune 500* companies.

Greenwood is currently president of Wave 9 Enterprises, Inc. and Career Consultants, two firms that specialize in strategic planning for careers and businesses, public relations and marketing. He is chairman of the board of Children On The Go, Inc., of which he is co-founder. He serves on the boards of directors of a major bank holding company and its lead bank, and an advertising/public relations agency.

In addition to writing HOW TO LAND YOUR FIRST JOB & MAKE A SUCCESS OF IT, he is co-author of THE NAME OF THE GAME IS LIFE. His writings also include a syndicated newspaper column, *Common Sense At Work©*.

Those who know Ramon Greenwood and seek his counsel are likely to describe him in such terms as "realistic" and "down-to-earth." They say, "He puts his experiences to work with an eye to results. He has the ability to make even the most complicated and formidable issues seem less forbidding and more manageable."

TABLE OF CONTENTS

Part Two – (Continued)

PREFACE

This book has been published because I believe it will help you and untold numbers of other young men and women make a successful entry into the world of full-time employment.

Unfortunately, I cannot guarantee such results. There are many factors, including luck, that enter into the equation of matching your assets with the needs of an employer. The same applies to what you do with your opportunities once you are on the job. But I can assure you that the guidelines and ideas presented in this book are based on common sense and they work. To the extent you employ them, you will be ahead of most of the competition you will face in your career.

Although I have researched the information presented here as to its accuracy and completeness, I cannot guarantee that this book is free of errors. I apologize now for any errors committed by omission or commission. If I have slighted anyone it was done unintentionally. Any and all shortcomings are attributed to me.

I have devoted a great deal of time, and no small amount of concern, to the matter of gender. In my opinion no satisfactory word has been coined to represent both sexes. The repeated use of he or she, his or hers, man or woman soon gets to be awkward and time consuming. I have opted in most instances for the gender most writers still seem to favor, the male. I believe my five granddaughters, whom I love and respect beyond description for who they are and the persons they will become, will attest to the fact that my choice of gender in this and all instances is free of prejudice.

Many people over the course of many years have made contributions to the writing of this book. Those contributions have been in many forms: experiences provided, wisdom imparted and ideas shared. Most important of all, there has been my family, every member of which has provided encouragement, consistently packaged in love, patience and understanding.

It is not possible to acknowledge all who have contributed, but I cannot commit this book to print without recognizing those who were on the first team.

My first thanks go to my family. They are Martha Holmes Greenwood, my wife; Mark Greenwood and Melissa Riemer, our son and daughter. They were my constant sources of encouragement in the writing of this book as they are in all things in life that matter. Cynthia Greenwood, Mark's wife, has done a splendid job editing the manuscript and in marketing the book. I have learned a great deal about how to manage a career from Jeff Riemer, our son-in-law.

I am indebted to Ray Holloway, human resources executive at International Paper Company; and to Rob Anderson and Stephanie Scheckelhoff, recent entries in the job market, who provided valuable insight from their special perspectives.

Lyndel Dean, vice president and associate creative director, at Cranford Johnson Robinson Woods, designed the book. Nancy Griebel, also of CJRW, managed the production. Lela Delgado was the typographer. They did first-class work, which is most appreciated.

Ramon Greenwood

INTRODUCTION

YOUR CHALLENGE

You are rapidly coming up on one of the most important and toughest challenges of your life. It is the moment of truth you have been moving toward since you first entered school.

It is time to land your first full-time job and make a success of it.

You will not be surprised to find this is not a simple and easy task. Buckle your seatbelt. It may get a bit bumpy for awhile. But you can come through the trip in good shape.

You are in for a cultural change. Shock may be a more accurate word. You will be leaving a rather comfortable world where as an upperclassman you have been a tribal elder. For a time now you will be just one of the Indians, and a young one at that. You have to get through the rite of passage.

You have been nurtured in a caring environment. Members of the faculty wanted you to succeed. Assignments have been straightforward: study this text; conduct this experiment; take this examination. Success has been easily measured. Choices have been well defined.

Time frames have been measured by semesters, holidays and the finite ending of school. Going forward, your future will be measured in decades of an evolving career.

Most students have reasonably good support systems composed of parents, friends and relatives going for them.

Now, you are facing a less-forgiving system. Your activities will be measured on the basis of ROI (return on investment.) The equation will change from "what can I do for you?" to "what have you done for me?".

Based on all you have witnessed and heard, this new world may not look very inviting.

Don't underestimate the competition for jobs. It is hot and heavy. In the decade of the '90s, colleges are turning out four-year graduates at a rate of over one million per year. (There were 1.2 million members of the class of '94.) Add to this number the master's degrees and doctorates that are awarded each year. The nation's high schools are handing out well in excess of three million diplomas each year. Presumably the vast majority of these young men and women are in the market for a job. Other graduates from earlier years are seeking to change jobs or recover from job losses. All of these people are your competitors.

At the same time, as you are aware from the daily news, the market for jobs, particularly in the ranks of early and middle range management, is undergoing dramatic if not traumatic changes. The market is shrinking. At the same time, it is changing in terms of its requirements. There are more applicants for good jobs than there are good jobs.

Time was when a college graduate with almost any kind of respectable credentials could count on walking off the campus straight into a job. Usually there were many options available. This is no longer the case. This is a buyers' market and it is likely to remain so for many years to come.

You cannot afford to let this situation discourage you, no matter how formidable and stressful it may seem now. Unless your favorite rich uncle died and left you the farm, or you hit the jackpot in the lottery:

you want a job, you must have a job

if you are going to get the things out of life you desire.

Remember, you only need one job from the many on the market. The key to a successful search is your being willing to go all out with an aggressive, well-thought-out marketing plan. Your objective is to find the match where what you have to sell fits with what a buyer wants to buy. A distinct advantage goes to those who work hardest at landing that job they want. The operative mode is aggressive, tenacious and proactive.

According to *Fortune* magazine, "80% or so of those who look for employment find work within six months..." The U. S. Department of Labor reports that the average job seeker will spend 20 weeks looking for a job. That is about one month longer than it took in the early 1990s.

GO FOR THE JOB YOU WANT

You can probably get a job of some kind if you go along with the herd of job seekers. But will it be the job you really want?

There is a certain degree of parity among people coming out of school and entering the job market. Most college graduates are adequately prepared in an academic sense to perform the basic tasks required in the field of work they have chosen. Of course, there are standouts in every class, but the vast majority of graduates are about on par with mixtures of strengths and weaknesses.

Grades cannot be ignored, but GPA is not the central issue in getting a job for most graduates. It is true that some of the "blue chip" companies absolutely set grades in the upper reaches (at least the top quartile) as the price for admission to an initial interview, particularly in such fields as engineering and accounting. On the other hand, recruiters tend to pay less attention to the GPA in the liberal arts type jobs and where smaller companies are concerned. In fact, many who have been successful in job searches report that they were never asked about their grades.

If grades were the "killer," the vast majority of graduates would never get a job.

Obviously, however in any case, it does help to have a GPA at a respectable level.

Recruiters such as Lew Shumaker, who heads college relations at DuPont, told *Fortune* magazine that he and his professional counterparts seek "students who are adaptable and agreeable enough to thrive in a diverse and ever-changing workplace, and committed to learning throughout their careers."

Other decision makers say that what counts most are demonstrated leadership; involvement in campus activities, particularly those related to a career field; and, always, experience.

Ray Holloway, a human resources development official at International Paper Company, says that his company doesn't recruit anyone below the top 25 percent GPA. Yet, he goes on to say that GPA is the "second best indicator of success." Attributes he calls "street smarts" count for the most during the interview and later on the job.

The point is that while one has to assume at least a passing performance in the classroom, more than academic preparation is required to successfully deal with the challenges of making a successful launch in the real work world. It is virtually impossible to overstate the importance of participation in campus organizations – especially professional societies – and of serving internships.

But in the final analysis, the keys to success are how you market yourself and how effective you are in applying what you have learned in school to getting things accomplished on the job once you are at work.

Unfortunately, little in the average person's education or training fully prepares him or her to meet these requirements.

College placement offices and career counselors in general do a good job, but their time and resources are necessarily limited and they are dealing with a lot of people. Therefore, in the normal course of events, much of what they can provide tends to be generic. This means that only a small minority of the students who enter the job market are fortunate enough to have any customized, individualized counseling on the realities of the maiden job search and what it is really like on that first full-time job. However, the amount and quality of help you get from these professionals is squarely up to you. Learn to work this system for all it is worth. You will be pleasantly surprised at the response you get when you demonstrate you are serious about your job search, you have a plan, and you need their help.

YOU HAVE AN ADVANTAGE

You already have a decided advantage in this competition because you recognize you need help in landing the job that is right for you and in making the most of the opportunity once you get it. So you are reading this book which is written to help you achieve this goal.

As much as I would like to see every first-time job seeker benefit from the contents of my book, the truth is that only a relatively small number will. Not everyone is dedicated to launching a successful career and willing to work to make it happen.

Some believe opportunity will come to their door and knock it down. Others just want to float, taking whatever job they can obtain just to get by. They think the "good" life of college will go on forever. Many are gridlocked by fear of graduating because it means the definite end of a known world and the beginning of an unknown universe.

Most of your competitors in the job market who are looking will use a lot of traditional tactics that are wasteful of time and energy. They will flood the market with old-fashioned resumes and hope.

(FLASH: IF YOU ARE PREPARING A TRADITIONAL RESUME, **STOP**! SAVE YOUR ENERGY. FINISH READING THIS BOOK BEFORE YOU EXPEND ONE MORE MINUTE ON A RESUME. I WILL EXPLAIN THAT LATER.

(IN FACT, PLEASE READ THE ENTIRE BOOK AT LEAST ONCE BEFORE PROCEEDING ANOTHER STEP WITH YOUR JOB SEARCH. THEN EXECUTE THE RECOMMENDED ACTIONS THAT ARE LAID OUT FOR YOU STEP BY STEP.)

Most job seekers will answer "help wanted" ads. They will depend on tips from Uncle Henry, who probably hasn't been in the job market for 30 years. Their objective will be a job...any job.

Meanwhile, you will be prepared to conduct a focused, organized campaign, the objective of which is the just-right job that will launch you on a rewarding career.

YOU CAN BE OPTIMISTIC

You can be optimistic about the endeavor you are about to undertake. There are employers looking at this very time for what you can provide if you have your act together and are willing to work.

Nothing is 100 percent guaranteed in life, but you can increase the odds in your favor if you will follow the guidelines and advice revealed in the following pages. There you will learn how to *seize control of your search* for the job you want, even in this volatile market. Then, when you land that job you will have a running start at making a success of it.

HOW TO LAND YOUR FIRST JOB & MAKE A SUCCESS OF IT is divided into two parts. The first section provides all of the information you will need to prepare the marketing plan that will help you identify the job you want, as well as the sales materials and tactics you will need to make that job yours. Yes, I said a marketing plan. Your chances for a successful search are increased by a quantum leap when you begin to think of yourself as a product to be packaged and sold. No offense intended. Consider yourself a can of soup. You are the marketing manager. The better your plan, in concept and execution, for packaging and presenting yourself the more likely you are to make a sale to the buyer of your choice.

Recently, a young lady came to visit with me concerning her search for a job. Frustration and worry were written all over her face. She had just graduated from a major university with a master's degree in marketing.

"I have been trying very hard," she said. "I have sent out resumes by the dozens and received very few responses. I have followed up on tips about possible openings. I'm not getting anywhere."

She wanted a job in marketing with a consumer goods company. A native of Arkansas, she hoped to live in Dallas.

"You need a marketing plan," I advised. "This plan ought to identify the kind of job you want and the conditions you want to work under,

6

even the place you want to live. Then it should spell out the assets you have to offer. It should spot candidate employers that constitute the market for your product. Finally, your marketing plan ought to contain a sales campaign to bring your product to the buyers' attention."

It was as if a light bulb had been turned on in a dark room.

"That's what I need," she said. "A marketing plan. I am a marketing major. Why didn't I think of that?"

Well, it is difficult to be objective and see yourself as a can of soup at this point or anytime in your life.

THE WAY IT REALLY WORKS

The second section of this book is your manual for the way the world of work really works. It is composed of 30 chapters. Each deals with Common Sense At Work© insights. Together, they will provide you with a head start on doing your job and making the dynamics of the employer organization work for you.

How important is this first job and your career?

Well, first there is the matter of economic necessity. But more is involved. In our culture we are identified and positioned by our work. In large measure, our jobs are who we are. I am an accountant. I am a chemical engineer. I am a salesperson.

In short, choosing the right career, making the right career moves at the right time, and working effectively in each phase of your career – from the first job through retirement – are keys to your personal well-being and financial success.

Read on. Take to heart the advice and guidelines provided here. Seize control of your career and your life today. Prepare your marketing plan. Employ persuasive sales tactics and materials. Get that job you desire. Make a success of it. Use your first full-time job to launch the career that will produce what you want for your life.

It's your life. Make the most of it.

Here's to your success!

PART ONE

CREATE YOUR OWN MARKETING PLAN

The issue we are dealing with is not your getting *just any* job. You should not have to settle for a consolation prize. *The objective is to get the job you want – the one that will launch you on a lifetime of satisfying work – under the conditions you want.*

In order to accomplish this goal in the most expeditious manner possible, you should put aside a great deal of what you have probably come to accept as the common wisdom about how to get a job. Much of that folklore will lead you to waste time and effort as you run helter-skelter without a defined plan of action. Besides, the odds are against you in terms of reaching your full potential if you become one of the herd, using the same old and tired tactics that most other job-seekers still employ.

A mass sales campaign with a flurry of traditional resumes, following up on tips from your parents' next-door neighbor, *may* get a job for you in these tough, competitive times, but it will likely be a lottery pick. You take what comes up on the draw.

You don't want to settle for being a part of the cattle call, do you?

By following the guidelines provided in this book, you can seize control and direct the process of landing your first full-time job to your advantage. Furthermore, you will have a head start in making the most of your lifetime of work.

To bring your search to the best possible conclusion, you need *a specific customized marketing plan* that will maximize your marketability. With such a plan, you can fuse what you have to offer with the unique needs and culture of an employer of your choice. Then everyone wins.

Begin your campaign today with a great sense of urgency. I know that may be hard to do. You can find a lot of reasons (i.e. excuses) to put off getting started. You may say, "I can put this off, I have plenty of time." After graduation, you can use the excuse that you have been in school a long time and you deserve a break. Or you may rationalize that it is such a big task that it is difficult to know where to begin.

Recognize that fear and inertia are your big enemies. For many people, graduation is a frightening prospect that freezes them into inaction. That is not surprising since it is the defined ending of one known world and the beginning of an unknown one. You can't afford to let fear and inertia take control. Step up right now and assume responsibility for your career. Ideally, you will have begun the process of getting your first job at least by the start of your junior year in college. But most people don't.

Whatever your situation, it is never too early or too late to get going.

I hope it doesn't come as a shock, but the market has not put everything on hold, waiting anxiously for you to become available. It would be a rare occurrence if the market came chasing after you with just the right job.

Don't fall into the trap that snared Peter Rogers.

After several years in the service he returned to college to earn a master's degree. When asked what he planned to do, his answer was definite and somewhat defiant: "I have been going to school and serving in the Army for almost all of my life. I am going to take some time off. I have a good education, plus my experience in the service. Someone will want to hire me."

I advised him that he was making a mistake.

"Among other things, in addition to the fact that you are on par with a lot of other people as far as education and experience are concerned," I said, "when you do decide to go after a job, you will have to explain this period of downtime. The interviewers will have to wonder if you couldn't get a job, or if you are hiding something, or if you lack a sense of urgency and ambition."

He ignored the advice. When he did get going it was with the kind of effort his attitude clearly predicted. He stumbled along without an organized effort. He sent out resumes, which were by necessity thin. Follow-ups didn't happen. He went off in several directions on the advice of relatives, college friends and friends of friends.

Things got to a critical state before he found employment. It was a job he did not want in a place where he didn't want to live. The result was a very unhappy young man.

The lessons, duplicated many times over, are clear. Get ahead of the game. Make your plans and start executing them today.

You are in a buyers' market. If you do not land a job while still in college *(and most people don't),* you need to get busy with your campaign your first day out of academia.

If you take a part-time job make it one that leaves you with plenty of flexible time to execute your job search. Get your priorities in order. Getting your first full-time job is a full-time job.

PLAN YOUR LIFE TO SUIT YOURSELF

Let's focus on one basic consideration before we proceed with guidelines for developing your own marketing plan.

It is absolutely essential that you make your plans reflecting your own thoughts about the kind of job you want. It is your life, your success and your happiness you are dealing with. It's up to you to make it happen. Don't go after a job just to please someone else. Following a family tradition, staying close to home to placate Mom and Dad may make them happy. There's no question that your going with IBM or General Electric could give your parents more bragging rights than if you join forces with SmallTime Computers. It is possible you could be just as satisfied by pleasing others first, but don't count on it. These sorts of influences and rewards based on the interests of others tend to wear thin after awhile. A career that challenges and satisfies you lasts a lifetime.

OVERCOME THE FEAR OF PLANNING

What's the problem with planning?

Why do so many of us act as if we can drift along day to day, thinking somehow we can achieve our dreams of success without having defined our personal goals and made plans to reach them?

Would any of us begin a trip across the country, or even across town, without setting the final destination, even if getting there involves some meandering around to enjoy the scenery? Would you or I think of building a house without knowing where we wanted to locate it; how many rooms it would contain; what construction materials would be used; and how much it would cost? Of course, we wouldn't.

A look at some of the reasons we fail to complete this vital task will help you to understand and to overcome the roadblocks that get in the way of effective planning.

The number one reason most of us don't set goals, assess our assets and make plans for our careers is *fear*. We are afraid that if we set goals and don't reach them we will be seen as failures. We are afraid to commit ourselves for fear we will go down the wrong road to a dead end of frustration and unhappiness from where there is no escape. We dread the accountability inherent in a stated goal.

Or we simply may not believe that it is possible to plan ahead. We tell ourselves, "there are just too many variables and imponderables in life."

We don't think a plan is necessary. What will be will be.

Wrong! To paraphrase the legendary merchant J. C. Penney, "Give me a stock clerk with a goal and I will give you a successful manager. Give me a stock clerk without a plan and I will give you a stock clerk."

According to Zig Ziglar, the great motivational speaker, research conducted by an Ivy League university knocks the props out from under those who deny the essentiality of planning. He reports that a survey of one graduating class determined that only three percent of the young men and women had taken all of the necessary steps to set out career goals and plans; 10 percent had done some of the necessary things; 87 percent had done very little or nothing. A follow-up study 20 years later revealed the three percent had accomplished more than the remainder of the class combined in terms of career positions and financial rewards.

One roadblock we encounter is that we feel we have so many options – so many things we can do and want to do – that we can't decide among them. We are like the proverbial blind dog in the meat locker.

Of course, it is difficult to get started. We may be paralyzed by the feeling that our hopes and dreams are just so enormous that they are beyond reach. The *gap* between where we are and where we want to be may seem to be more than we can cross. The first steps look totally insignificant in the light of the journey to be accomplished. So we sit on the starting blocks without a road map, mesmerized by our dreams and overawed by the enormity of it all.

All of these reasons (they are really excuses) for not setting goals can be dealt with when we knuckle down to the demanding step-by-step process that planning requires.

If groundless fears are holding you back, they must be exorcised before you will be able to create your marketing plan. If you are afraid to commit yourself by setting goals, remember they need not impose an irrevocable life sentence. Nothing is forever. Once upon a time an employer was thought of as a partner "till death do us part." Not any more. The average job over the course of a career lasts seven years. First jobs have an average life time of far less than that.

Research conducted by Duke University's Fuqua School of Business among 1994 MBA graduates at 11 top B-schools found that only five percent expect to work for their first employer for their full careers. Nearly half plan to work less than five years in their first job.

It may seem paradoxical, but good planning takes into account the fact that new circumstances may dictate changes of course along the way. It is all right to switch goals if your notions of what you want to achieve move in other directions, or if the environment changes. However, it is not healthy to change goals if you are running away from obstacles and hard work.

TAKE TIME TO GET ORGANIZED

You are about to launch on a major undertaking that will have an enormous impact on your life now and for years to come. Get organized in three basic areas before proceeding so you can make the best use of your time and resources. First, organize the process for handling information and developing your campaign. Second, organize your search team. Third, organize your sources of information.

Organize The Process

You will save time and avoid frustration later if you take time at the outset to get organized to effectively utilize your time and the data you develop as your campaign moves along.

First, you will need a place to serve as your campaign head-quarters. It can be your desk in your dorm room. Maybe it is the kitchen table in your apartment or at home where you are living temporarily. It doesn't matter so long as it is the place you *go to work.*

It will be necessary to keep detailed information about the candidate employers you will identify and all contacts with them from step one to closure of a deal. This means having complete, easily retrievable records about the organization and persons contacted, when contacts were made, discussions that ensued and conclusions reached.

Access to a computer is absolutely essential because you are going to be customizing your campaign into various configurations in order to zero in on individual targets.

Another essential tool is an answering machine. You can't afford to sit at your campaign headquarters waiting on telephone calls.

You will need to set up easily retrievable files, one for each candidate company. These files will contain the information developed about each company: industry ratings, sales, number of employees, acquisitions, legal problems, product development, recent changes in management, outlooks for growth, industry trends, honors, anything that will provide you with an insight into the company's business.

Each file will also contain information about the locations where they have operations and in which you would like to live.

One of those old-fashioned brown accordion-type paperboard file cases in which many manila files can be stored will work well.

Organize Your Search Team

You should organize your own personal job search team.

Perhaps without realizing it, you started early in your college days, if not before, to come in contact with a number of people who can be of assistance to you in your maiden job search as well as later in your career. It is now time to expand that resource and organize your campaign to utilize this network.

This support team can be of great help all along the way in defining your goals, assessing your strengths and weaknesses, making your plans, and securing the job you want. Use them as you feel the need and as common sense dictates. You can set up your team as you see fit, but for best results it should be made up of a variety of players.

Faculty members and key people in the college placement office can be crucial to your campaign. So can men and women of reputation and authority in your chosen field with whom you can network beyond the campus.

If you have not been able to decide on a career field, common sense will tell you how you should extend the makeup of your search apparatus to include influentials with broader experience rather than relying entirely on those identified with a specific field.

All of this sounds like a formidable task, and it is, but you will be surprised how it will fall in place once you get started.

Almost always, if you seek help from the sort of people you need on your team, and you do it in the right way, you will get a positive response.

Human nature comes into play. People have their own vested interests in helping other people. They may expect help in return some day. They may assist others because it is good for their ego or their own material positions. They may do it out of sincere interest in a particular profession or in young people in general. Or their aid may be forthcoming for a combination of these and other reasons. It doesn't make any difference. Establish your support team, and put the full squad to work.

Let's assume you have defined the job you want to go for. You should use your search network to run a check on it against the realities of the work world. What's the size of the market for the job you want? How much competition is there? Where are the jobs? What will it take to get the job you want? What levers can you pull to make your search the most effective it can be? What will it actually be like working in this field?

These questions will change, of course, if you are still considering various options as to the field in which you want to start. You will be seeking information about opportunities, working conditions, and requirements in a variety of markets.

In any case, use your search team as a source of information and advice. It may also prove to be helpful in providing encouragement if the going gets rough, as it may very well before you are securely attached to someone's payroll.

Of course, you already have your friends and relatives on your team. They want you to succeed and they will be willing to help. But, frankly, they are not always the best source of objective advice.

Enlist The Faculty

There may have been times during your college years when you would doubt the adage that "college professors are human, too." However, the truth is that most of them are human with generous egos. Go ahead, make them feel good. Solicit their advice; tap into their knowledge and contacts; recruit them as mentors. Don't hesitate to polish the apple.

Not only can members of the faculty be of great assistance during your search for that first job, they can be helpful for many years to come. Most of them, if approached properly, will be glad to support your campaign. After all, it is the rare individual, including the college professor, who doesn't like to be asked to lend his expertise and contacts on behalf of a worthy person. In addition, the placement of a student with an employer earns points for the professor involved. (Who knows when that employer may need a consultant? Or the professor may want to place an intern or use the resources of the employer for some research project.)

The better members of the faculty know key people in the fields in which they specialize and teach. Many of them serve as consultants; they often speak at professional and trade conventions. They write books for these markets.

Recruiters maintain contact with relevant faculty members of the colleges they recruit from, and will often call them for recommendations before and after contacting students. Furthermore, if you have a key faculty member on your side, he may become proactive and contact potential employers for you.

Consider the potential positive impact and benefits of these remarks from a faculty member to a recruiter:

"Oh, yes, Jane Jones is a fine student, one of my best. She has demonstrated a real interest beyond the classroom in making a career in marketing. She is constantly looking for information about her field."

"John Smith is one of my brightest students. He has been assisting me in my work with our professional society."

The obvious place to begin enlisting faculty members into your apparatus is in their classrooms. But you can and should go beyond that setting. Visit with them in their offices and over coffee in the lounge. Discuss your aspirations and your plans. One recent graduate suggests that it is a good idea to establish a close relationship with at least one new professor each semester.

The value of internships cannot be overstated, and they are gaining in importance each year. Try to line up these and other opportunities to gain experience and learn more about your field while solidifying relationships.

Faculty members can provide useful guidance on activities such as volunteer work and participation in professional organizations and conferences that will provide contacts and knowledge helpful to your career.

Use The Placement Office

The effectiveness of placement offices varies greatly. Some may be no more than a reference library and repository of resumes. Others may be aggressive in searching out recruiters and opportunities.

Use the one available to you whatever the case.

Although you won't be in a position to actually activate the placement office on your campus until your senior year, get to know the staff members far in advance of this time, at least by the end of your junior year.

Take advantage of the career library. Talk with career advisors. Review your goals with them at an early date. Ask them the same sort of questions you are asking faculty members. Remember, these people will be the ones who can provide advance information and help with scheduling interviews with recruiters who visit your campus. They also will be contacted by recruiters for leads on promising students.

Later, they can help you to hone your interviewing skills.

Tap Into The Network Of Influentials

Networking among *influentials* in your field beyond the faculty and staff at the placement office is a key part of your search apparatus and subsequent career development. Never mind that "networking" sometimes has a bad image. It brings up visions of social-climbing and the old fraternity and sorority ties. Serious, mature networking is making contacts and exchanging information and influences that advance a common or shared interest. Although abused sometimes, networking among people with influence and knowledge is good business, common sense at work.

Influentials fall into three groups. They are leaders in your chosen field; people of wisdom and power; and literally anyone with a range of contacts.

Selected leaders in your chosen field can provide you with helpful insights and information, and, eventually perhaps, contacts. So can men and women who possess wisdom about careers and the world in general. The latter group are especially important if you are undecided on your career path. The third category for networking is literally anyone you can meet who "gets around." (You never know who has a lead you can capitalize on.)

You already know how to contact and activate members of your faculty and placement network. Making contact with the influentials in your career field and people of influence in general may be more difficult, but it can be done.

You have probably heard of certain influentials in your community or in your intended field of work whom you would like to ask for information and advice. Faculty members can be helpful in identifying other such individuals. Your reading of the newspapers and trade literature will help you identify others. Friends and relatives can make helpful suggestions.

Don't be bashful. Go for the real influentials. A list of 12 prospects is a good place to start. If you are persuasive (or lucky) you may get to see two or three out of the 12. That would be a good start.

If friends, relatives or faculty/placement officers personally know any of the individuals on your list, ask them to arrange an introduction. If an introduction is not possible, ask for permission to use that person's name. Faculty members can be particularly helpful in this exercise. If you are not able to establish a direct link, make the contacts without connections.

Write a personal letter to the individual you want to visit. If a contact has been made on your behalf, or if there is a connection of some kind acknowledge these facts in your letter. State frankly that you are seeking career advice, not a job at this point, and that you know the person whom you are contacting can be immensely helpful. Ask for an interview not to exceed 30 minutes. Say you will follow up with a call to that person's secretary.

(Later in this book you will find suggestions about this letter, as well as how to conduct informational interviews and follow-ups with these key people.)

Organize Your Sources

To carry out the kind of customized, focused marketing campaign envisioned in this book, you will need to compile a great deal of information about career fields, industries, specific companies and locations. Fortunately, there is no shortage of information for this exercise. Your challenge is to learn how to tap into it and organize your data so that it can be put to work for you.

The following are a few of the many directories found in college placement, public or school libraries from which you can develop in-depth files on economic sectors and individual organizations.

- *The Million Dollar Directory* from Dun and Bradstreet
- *Thomas Register of American Manufacturers*
- *Register of Corporations, Directors and Executives* from Standard and Poor's
- *North American Register of Business & Industry*

In addition, there are many other related directories that will be sources of important information, including:

- *Dun's Employment Opportunities Directory – The Career Guide*
- *Encyclopedia of Careers and Vocational Guidance*
- *Dictionary of Occupational Titles*
- *Encyclopedia of Job Descriptions*
- *Occupational Outlook Handbook*

There is a wealth of information in the annual directories of the top 500 industrial corporations and the top 500 service corporations in America published each year by *Fortune* magazine. *Business Week* produces an excellent report four times each year which details the performance of 900 American businesses. *Forbes* prepares a similar report.

In addition, there are annual reports that every publicly-owned company must produce for its shareholders. These companies also are obligated to produce various reports for government agencies, including 10-Q and 10-K reports. You can get copies of these reports upon request to the Office of The Corporate Secretary at each company. These documents may also be available in your library. Incidentally, when you contact the corporate secretary's office, request other information that this person may feel will help you better understand the company.

Of course, there are many business publications loaded with good information about current news developments in specific companies, as well as in the industry, and economic trends that impact them. These publications include *The Wall Street Journal, Business Week, Fortune, Barron's, Nation's Business, Inc., Forbes* and many more. Copies, including back issues, can be found at your library.

Trade associations can provide a wealth of information. Each industry underwrites several of them. You can get the names of these organizations from your public library or college placement office.

Electronic data banks such as CompuServe, Nexis, DataTimes, America On-Line, and Internet are also good sources.

Almost every town and state has a chamber of commerce or a tourism development office that would be happy to provide you with information about living conditions. Banks and newspapers can be good sources of this type of information, too.

MAKE YOUR PLAN NOW

You have organized your systems and your search infrastructure. It is time to start creating your marketing and sales plan.

There are four steps in a good planning process. They are simply Common Sense At Work©.

1. The first step in creating your marketing plan is to define what kind of job you want. Keep in mind a critical subsidiary question: What purpose do you want that first job to serve in getting to where you want to be, say three to five years from now?

2. The second step is to determine where you are now. What assets do you possess in terms of education, skills and interests?

3. The third step is to look at your immediate goal (i.e. the job you want). Having analyzed where you are now and where you want to go, you can clearly see the gap that exists between the two points.

4. The fourth step is to devise a marketing plan which spells out the actions you will take to bridge the gap.

STEP ONE: DEFINE THE JOB YOU WANT

It is worth repeating once again: your goal is not getting *just any job*. It is all about getting *the job you want, under the conditions you want, where you want to live.*

So, common sense says you should spell out in writing a firm definition of that first job and the kind of place in which you want to work. Don't be foolish. There are no perfect jobs. But go ahead, define your ideal job. You have a chance to get it. If your first choice is not available now, you can always back off a bit, take another course of action to secure the second or third most desirable position, and wait until number one opens up. Certainly, second or third choice in the league in which you want to work is better than letting your future go up for grabs in a sort of random mating.

WHAT TO EXPECT FROM YOUR EMPLOYER

Defining your choice job should include what you expect from your employer if you want to work in a positive environment where you can become a first class player.

Foremost, you should expect your employer to provide an environment of opportunity in which hard work and achievement are recognized and rewarded. This means a place where you will be encouraged to grow as fast as you can, broadening your capabilities and building your experience every step of the way. You want to work where you will be allowed to assume all the responsibilities you can handle.

This environment should allow you – no, encourage you – to take common sense risks with the assurance that you will be rewarded if you are right and not punished if you turn out to be wrong in a well-thought-out attempt.

You should expect an employer who provides you with the tools and resources needed to get your assignments done on time, in a manner that produces results for the organization and satisfaction for you.

Continuing education should be just that – continuing.

The organization you want to work for should maintain a highly visible connection between efforts, achievements, and rewards. In other words, this means a place where you can share in the rewards of a compensation package that is at the top end of the range as measured against competitors in your line of work in the market where you live. There is little incentive to make your best effort where the compensation review always results in across-the-board, cost-of-living raises for one and all alike, loafers as well as producers; where winners are never singled out for pats on the back and cash in the pocket.

Over time, the absence of opportunity, the lack of resources and the failure to reward good work will kill the fire in even the most ambitious of us. These failures will also cripple organizations. You do not want to launch your career in this kind of environment.

To maximize your chances for success at work you should find an employer who embodies most of the following characteristics:

- Delivers quality products and services of which you can be proud.
- Has a history of profitable growth.
- Provides a good physical environment in which to work.
- Develops people and promotes from within; provides growth opportunities.
- Has earned a reputation as a good corporate citizen.
- Has well-established and visible personnel policies.
- Has demonstrated a willingness and ability to change with the times.
- Practices two-way communications with its employees, its customers and its neighbors.

You will want an employer who embraces a motivational system that Herbert Korthoff, chief executive officer of Wright Technology, describes as "respect, recognition and remuneration."

SELECT THE CANDIDATE EMPLOYERS

Having defined the characteristics you want your employer to possess, you should determine the type of organization in which you would like to work. The following questions are intended to provide a starting point for such an exercise. You will want to expand on the exploration. Be as specific as possible. For example, if your interest is in the food sector, specify whether you are interested in food service, food retailing or food production. (This will be a helpful exercise even if you have a firm idea of where you want to work. It will help you validate your decision or it just might cause you to take a fresh look.)

What sector of the economy do I want to work in?

Academia	_____
Advertising/public relations	_____
Aerospace/defense	_____
Automotive	_____
Banks	_____
Computers	_____
Construction	_____
Consumer products	_____
Consulting	_____
Electronics	_____
Food	_____
Energy	_____
Health care	_____
Housing	_____
Leisure time	_____
Manufacturing	_____
Metals and mining	_____
Non-bank financial	_____
Not-for-profit	_____

Paper and forest products   _____

Publishing and broadcasting   _____

Public service   _____

Retailing   _____

Services   _____

Telecommunications   _____

Transportation   _____

Utilities   _____

Other   _____

What type of organization do I want to work in?

Large corporation   _____

Small privately-owned company   _____

Start-up entrepreneurship   _____

Self-employment   _____

Public service   _____

Government agency   _____

Professional partnership   _____

Other   _____

What kind of work do I want to do/am I prepared for?

Administrative   _____

Sales/marketing   _____

Manufacturing   _____

Technical   _____

Financial   _____

Advertising/public relations   _____

Data processing   _____

Other   _____

Where do I want to live?
(Be as specific as possible in identifying the area where you want to live.)

Northeast	_____
Southeast	_____
South	_____
Midsouth	_____
Midwest	_____
Southwest	_____
Rocky Mountains	_____
West Coast	_____

What lifestyle do I want?

Urban	_____
Small town	_____
Outdoor recreational opportunities in abundance	_____
Cultural/educational opportunities in abundance	_____
Other	_____

With the completion of this exercise you should have a clearer profile of your desired employer.

If, after you have completed these exercises, you are uncertain or have no idea of the kind of job you want, the following section will be helpful to you in achieving the kind of focus you need for a successful search.

SET A MEGA-GOAL

Once you have defined the job you want, you should put a mega-goal in writing. Be specific. It won't do to define the driver goal as "I will be successful." Within reasonably broad parameters, the goal should say how successful, doing what, where you want to work and live.

Time frames are critical. Three years out is about right. As you set goals, establish checkpoints in time along the way. Make sure you meet them.

An example of a mega-goal could be: "By (*date*), I will be a brand manager in a major consumer goods company. I will be earning $XXX. I will have reduced my student loan debt by X percent." (You may want to include location of the job. This depends on how important this consideration is in your ambitions.)

It is a good idea to set a stretch goal, but not an unrealistic one.

It is also desirable to define a number of subsidiary or enabling goals, each with a due date, that relate to the big target. Your subsidiary goals might be such achievements as earning an advance degree, learning to play golf, or becoming an accomplished public speaker. Go ahead and spell them out, but don't take your eyes off the prize.

The goal-setting process should include a realistic explanation of why each goal is important. What will be the payoff? What will be the personal benefits in terms of lifestyle, family impact and other value?

STEP TWO: DETERMINE WHERE YOU ARE NOW

The second step in the planning process is to realistically understand your current situation vis a vis your goals. What are your qualifications, your interests? What drives you?

Take an inventory; that is, complete a written analysis to determine what assets you have to offer for sale in the market you have chosen. Count your liabilities as well. Your assets include education, experience, attitudes, skills and interests. Be sure to take into account your experiences and what you have learned about your skills and interests from all of the jobs you have held both for pay and on a volunteer basis. Include the things you like to do, those tasks that light your fire. To round out the picture, list the liabilities. These are things you dislike doing, as well as those at which you have failed or where you are short on qualifications. Each of these items on the balance sheet of your life should be listed in considerable detail. You will find it helpful to use the *Personal Inventory and Balance Sheet* form that follows to organize your thoughts.

When you have completed this exercise, you will be able to see your demonstrated strengths and weaknesses in an organized and graphic form. Your likes and dislikes will also become apparent.

PERSONAL INVENTORY AND BALANCE SHEET
(Fill out one form for each employment situation, profit and not-for-profit)

Employer: _____

_____

Location: _____

Dates of Relationship: From _____ To _____

Position(s) Held: _____

_____

Significant Duties: _____

_____

_____

Significant Projects: _____

_____

_____

Skills Developed and Applied: _____

_____

_____

Application of Formal Education: _____

_____

_____

Significant Results Obtained: _____

_____

_____

Motivating Forces: _____

_____

_____

Recognitions Received: _____

_____

Activities Most Enjoyed: _____

_____

Activities Least Enjoyed: _____

_____

_____

Failures: _____

_____

Lessons Learned From Relationship: _____

_____

_____

_____

STEP THREE: DEFINE THE GAP

You have completed steps one and two in creating your own customized marketing plan. You have defined where you want to go (i.e. the job you want.) You have analyzed where you are now in terms of assets; that is, what you have to offer for sale.

Now you are ready for step three. Look first at your present situation and then at where you want to go. Obviously, there exists a *gap* between the two. It is time to turn your attention to what you must do to bridge that gap.

Again, put it in writing. The following form will be helpful in this important step of your planning process. Your best and total effort is needed for this exercise. This is not a time to be modest, nor is it a time to wear rose-colored glasses.

DEFINE THE GAP

My Current Situation:
Assets & Liabilities

(Use the information developed in the several PERSONAL INVENTORY & BALANCE SHEET forms you have completed to summarize your assets and liabilities.)

_____
_____
_____
_____
_____
_____
_____
_____
_____
_____

THE GAP

My Goal:
The Job I Want

(Use the information developed earlier in "Define The Job You Want" and "Set a Mega-Goal" to summarize your goal.)

_____
_____
_____
_____
_____
_____
_____
_____
_____

42

IT'S A TIME FOR REALISM

If you are going to build a sturdy bridge from where you are to where you want to go, it is time for a truth session. This is one of the most important steps in the entire process. Are the goals you have set realistic in terms of the assets you bring to the specified market? The positive thinking gurus not withstanding, just because you want a particular job doesn't mean you are qualified for it.

"Unrealistic expectations are the seedbed of depression," declares Zig Ziglar, the motivational counselor.

Can you get across the gap in the time frame in which you are dealing?

Stretch goals are healthy. They are to be encouraged. But stay with reality. If you set and reach big goals that force you to extend yourself, you will enjoy great satisfaction and success. If on the other hand, you go for goals that don't require your best, you will grow lazy and self-satisfied. If you aim for targets you have little chance of hitting, you are looking for frustration and pain.

Let's make the point with an extreme example. Under normal circumstances, it is not realistic to set a goal of being vice president of sales for a major organization as your first job. That is a challenging interim goal for your career, perhaps seven or eight years down the road on your way toward the presidency of your employer company. In the meantime your assets more likely are in line with a position of salesperson or sales trainee. (There is nothing wrong with that if the position provides you with a positive entry point for a successful career launch, doing what you want to do, with plenty of upside opportunity.)

The critical point is to go for the best first job you are qualified for at this point. If your basic assets don't get you where you really want to go, then decide what you have to do to acquire those assets that will. Your strategy for this undertaking is a subject for another time. For now, the challenge is to get that first job by matching your current assets with the best possible employment situation.

43

STEP FOUR: BRIDGE THE GAP

Go to the work sheet titled, "Defining The Gap." Write the following in the blank space under the heading, "The Gap":

I WILL BRIDGE THIS GAP BETWEEN WHERE I AM AND WHERE I WANT TO BE BY CREATING AND EXECUTING MY OWN CUSTOMIZED MARKETING PLAN. THIS PLAN WILL:

I.   BRING MY SPECIAL ASSETS IN THE MOST PERSUASIVE MANNER POSSIBLE TO THE ATTENTION OF CANDIDATE EMPLOYERS FOR WHOM I WANT TO WORK.

II. GAIN AN OPPORTUNITY TO PERSONALLY MEET THOSE POTENTIAL EMPLOYERS AND CONVINCE THEM THAT MY ASSETS CAN BE PUT TO WORK TO THEIR ADVANTAGE.

III. GET THE OFFER I WANT FROM AT LEAST ONE CANDIDATE EMPLOYER.

IV. CLOSE A DEAL.

V.   GET TO WORK WITH COMMON SENSE AS MY GUIDE IN DEVELOPING MY ASSETS AND PUTTING THEM TO WORK FOR MY BENEFIT.

DEVELOP YOUR SALES CAMPAIGN

You have completed the four preparatory steps required to develop your plan. This means you have set your goals, defining the kind of job you want. Furthermore, you have measured your assets; that is, you have determined what you have to offer a buyer (i.e. employer). These two actions have led you to recognize that there exists a gap between where you are and where you want to go. You have embraced the idea that the way to bridge this gap is to devise and execute a personal marketing plan that presents your package of goods to the most likely buyers in the most persuasive way so that one or more of them will be moved to acquire your services.

You are ready to move on to the preparation of your strategic marketing plan.

You may be short on experience. Welcome to the club. Most graduates are in the same boat. But chances are you have more applicable experience than you think. Your grades may not be the very best. But you can overcome these obstacles with a well-executed, creative and aggressive marketing plan.

You are not a commodity product to be sold in the mass market at the lowest going price, whatever that happens to be at the time. To repeat a point made earlier, you are not looking for *just any* job. You are going for that *best job,* the one that will put you in the field you want to be in, in the kind of company you want to work for, doing what you like best to do (and do best).

You are a unique product. You do not have to surrender to the currents and vagaries of the market. You can take control of the process.

The key (and it is no secret) to your making the sale is the same as in any other selling situation. *The nature and quality of the goods being offered for sale have to match the needs of a buyer.*

Remember, you are not hunting with a shotgun loaded with scatter shots. You need a rifle with a microscopic sight with which you are going to zero in on the bull's-eye where the fit between supply and demand exist. You can't reach out to the total universe of the job market, nor do you want to. You are looking for eagles and they don't fly in flocks.

So your task now is to target potential buyers (i.e. *candidate employers)* where there is a reasonable match between what you have to sell and what they need to buy. Once these potential buyers are on your screen of opportunity you can begin the mating process.

You can do this by taking the information you have compiled about the kind of job you want and can reasonably aspire to get. This is a simple procedure in terms of concept; however, it does require a considerable amount of basic research. Your objective at this point is to identify *a handful of potential employers* among the literally millions of places of employment that exist out there.

You should apply five screens in your selection of candidates:
(1) Sector of the economy in which you want to work.
(2) Type of organization in which you want to work.
(3) Kind of work you want to do on your first job.
(4) Where you want to live.
(5) Lifestyle you seek.

AN EXAMPLE OF THE TARGETING PROCESS

Let's create an imaginary scenario to see how the targeting process can work. Steve Morgan has a degree in accounting. He has determined he wants to begin his career in the paper industry. This indicates that he most likely will find his best opportunities in a large corporation. That is fine with Steve because he feels he would be best suited to working in a big organization. He would like to start in accounting and then move on to broader management responsibilities.

He grew up in Jackson, Tennessee, and earned his degree from the University of Illinois. He would like to live in a major city in Tennessee, close, but not too close to his home town.

Obviously, the next step for Steve is to identify organizations that fit the profile of his interests and desires; those that offer potential for growth in that first job and beyond.

To complete this step, he needs detailed information about the paper industry so that he can determine which companies have operations in Tennessee in or near a metro center within a reasonable distance from his hometown.

He can find a wealth of information about the pulp and paper industry in the *Lockwood-Post Directory of The Pulp, Paper and Allied Trades,* as well as in the broader-based sources listed earlier. The major association in the paper industry, the American Forest Products Association, headquartered in Washington, D. C., is also an excellent source.

When Steve has pinpointed specific candidate organizations he should run a parallel research project to assemble information about the living conditions in the several areas where these companies have operations. As cited previously, local chambers of commerce, libraries and reference books are the sources of mountains of information. Helpful information also can be obtained through a telephone call to a local bank or the local newspaper.

He should turn to his search team for input. What can they tell him about the paper industry? Do they have contacts that could be helpful? It is just possible that these discussions will identify attractive alternatives in other industries.

When Steve Morgan starts his search through these various files for information about companies in the paper industry, he will soon discover that there are at least 16 companies that meet his requirement of a "large corporation." Among the leaders in this group are International Paper Company, Georgia-Pacific, Kimberly-Clark, James River Corporation and Champion International.

He will find these companies have several operations in Tennessee and surrounding states.

With continued research to narrow the screen he will learn that International Paper Company (IP) has its major operating center in Memphis, Tennessee.

The company's annual report will reveal many other interesting facts. The company had sales of $13.7 billion with net earnings of $289 million in 1993 from a broad range of forest products. It employs 70,000 men and women in plants and forestlands in 26 countries. It spends $80 million a year or more on research. Its charitable foundation makes grants of well over $2 million per year. It has a strong environmental protection program.

Therefore, IP satisfies the basic criteria to qualify as a primary target.

ESTABLISH THREE TIERS OF CANDIDATES

A point that should be obvious must be underscored at this time. While the recommended strategies are aimed at enabling you to get that job you want, this is not to suggest that you should be foolish enough to put all your eggs in one basket. You cannot afford to get so hung up on one target that you let all the others go begging. Instead, you should use the process recommended here to establish at least three tiers of targets from "most desirable," to "very desirable," to "acceptable." Identify two or three candidate employers in the first tier and eight or 10 in the second tier for highly-focused individualized marketing campaigns. The third tier, the "acceptable" one should include 25 or more potentials.

Finally, so that you keep the maximum number of options open, it is a good idea to devote some attention to a broader scanning of the possibilities in addition to your three tiers. That is, listen to your contacts for leads that may not have occurred to you. Pick up tips from your reading of the daily news and trade journals. If these leads are within the scope of your goals, pursue them.

You may use more than one approach to identifying types of targets. Instead of the approach of a specific industry, you might identify targets as "large, publicly-owned corporations," or "not-for-profit public service organizations." Or you might let your selection of targets be governed by geographic location.

CREATE SALES MATERIALS

You are now ready to focus on developing an arsenal of sales material, the objective of which is to get attention and lead the person reviewing your information to conclude that there is enough of a possibility of a fit between what you have to offer and the employer's need to warrant an interview.

You improve your chance of reaching your goal by presenting your credentials in a different way so as to grab the recruiters' attention and actually make their job easier. This is not to suggest that you get "cute." Singing telegrams are out, unless you are seeking employment in a highly creative field such as copywriting at an advertising agency. It is to suggest, however, that you remember you are marketing a product.

Your basic package of sales materials should include at least these five items:

(1) Personal "calling" cards
(2) Personalized stationery
(3) Resume
(4) Overview of Qualifications
(5) Sales letters

EMPLOY DYNAMIC LANGUAGE

Think aggressively and positively when you are preparing all of your sales materials. Use action-packed, positive, confident, dynamic words in all of your communications. Forget the passive and tentative. People who phrase their outlook in terms of "I will try" accomplish less than those who declare "I will."

Your campaign materials ought to sparkle with such trigger words and terms as:

directed, created, supervised, achieved, reduced, increased, expanded, gained, attracted, motivated, reorganized, restructured, revitalized, sold, convinced, persuaded, grew, enlarged, simplified, innovated, stimulated, renewed, built, instructed, negotiated...

experienced, successfully concluded, exceeded goals, launched first, ahead of schedule, under budget, organized resources, took charge of, won awards, trained team, opened first office, led effort, trained others, managed campaign...

common sense, communications skills, entrepreneurial attitude, can handle pressure, willing to work hard, goal-oriented, willing to relocate, resourceful, demonstrated leadership, career-oriented, mature, can solve problems, results-oriented, practical, real-world experience, respect details, know how to listen and take directions, adaptable, learn quickly, outgoing personality, self-starter.

Cast all of your messages in terms of benefits to the employer. People act in terms of their own needs and what they perceive to be their best interests. The needs of potential employers are the only thing that counts in their minds. That is the dance the fiddler is playing, so get in step.

When you are creating your sales materials, visualize advertising copy that you see every day in the newspapers and on television. What are the messages? They are all consumer-oriented. Price, convenience, prestige, better life, success, profit, less worry, greater freedom, increased happiness, a better lifestyle and more.

The three top "product attributes" you can deliver to a buyer are education, attitude and experience.

The subject of experience always looms large. And it is difficult to deal with in most cases.

You may feel like you are in a "catch-22" world. Employers are looking for experience. But how can you get experience if you must have a job to get experience, and in order to get a job you must have experience?

Two facts prevail here.

One, of course employers would like entry-level job candidates with a great deal of experience, but they know they probably won't find many of them. Two, you probably have more experience than you realize. The challenge is to present that experience in the most favorable light.

For example, suppose you have mowed lawns and clipped shrubbery during your vacations, beginning with your junior year in high school. You can either present the idea that you "did lawn work" or that you "operated a lawn care service."

If you "did lawn work" you cranked up the lawn mower and mowed the grass. If you "operated a lawn care service" you marketed your services, you managed your equipment, you scheduled your work, you (might have) employed others, you (might have) bought your equipment.

Suppose you were student manager of the college football team. Did you just show up for the games, hand out towels and parade the team mascot on a leash? Or did you handle logistics for road trips, control the inventory of equipment, schedule tutorials and more?

A candidate employer may recognize that you are gilding the lily a bit, but your positive approach to the matter is likely to be appreciated so long as you are completely honest.

CREATE CARDS AND STATIONERY

An up-front investment in printing a supply of quality personal "calling" cards and personalized stationery will pay dividends. Don't bother with engraving. Just go to a good quick-print shop for these supplies. Select a good white bond paper stock, standard size of 8½ x 11 inches. If you want something a bit more distinctive you can use a light gray paper. No chartreuse or purple, please. Don't try to be clever with a knockout design. Ordinary typefaces and layout are best. Specify black or dark gray ink. Include the standard information of name, address, telephone and fax numbers on the first sheet of the stationery. Order a supply of "following sheets" printed with only your name at the top of the page.

Have a supply of mailing labels printed. You will need two sizes of envelopes, the number 10s for regular letters and 9 x 12s to mail your 8½ x 11 letters and other sales materials in flat configuration.

Your "business" card should include the basic name and address data. You may think the cards are a bit pretentious, but they are not. They will be especially useful when you are introducing yourself for interviews, both on and off campus.

PREPARE YOUR RESUME

Considerable controversy surrounds the subject of resumes, even though they have been standard fare since day one. Many of the big "blue chip" companies favor them. They mesh with their recruiting machinery, which given the volume of their annual searches and the torrent of resumes they receive, has to be automated to a considerable extent.

While a resume is a basic requirement in a well-rounded kit of sales materials, you should not rely on the traditional resume as the major piece in your campaign.

Consider for a moment all the resumes you have seen. Change the names of the applicants and their schools and the resumes all look alike. Now, think of the recruiters who must have nightmares about drowning in a flood of monotonous paper.

A resume is a resume is a resume. They are direct mail solicitations, turned out cookie-cutter style by the tens of thousands. They inundate the market. In his book RESUMES DON'T GET JOBS, Bob Weinstein reports that "AT&T and IBM receive over 1 million resumes a year."

Resumes yield a low rate of return. (It is instructive to recognize that professionals in the business of direct mail marketing are usually happy to get a two or three percent return from a mailing. It is a safe bet that resumes don't do any better.)

Always keep in mind that under most conditions resumes don't get jobs. At best, resumes get interviews. The same applies to all of the materials in your sales kit.

In the real world, resumes are frequently used as screening devices. Certain cutoff points are established (i.e. grades, schools attended, etc.) and they are applied by rote. So don't create a resume that provides a reason for you to be rejected. Create one instead that gets you past the gatekeepers.

Given the constraints of the format of the traditional resume, there is little room for more than a recitation of the barest facts. Therefore, there is scant opportunity to provide a cohesive rationale for selecting John Doe from the crowd.

Having made these negative points about traditional resumes, I still recommend that you prepare one for three reasons. First, this undertaking will be a good way to organize your vital information. Second, you may need a resume to apply to a candidate employer whose recruiting system demands such a presentation. Third, you will want to include a traditional resume in your sales package in some instances.

Many excellent books have been written on the subject of preparing resumes. A good selection of these are available in libraries and bookstores to which you have access. However, unless you want to do exhaustive research on the subject, the information provided in HOW TO LAND YOUR FIRST JOB & MAKE A SUCCESS OF IT provides the basic information you will need to prepare your resume.

While creativity is essential in the preparation of your sales letters and five-point qualification presentation (more about that later), resumes are another matter. The rule is to stick with the traditional.

Your resume should be:
- Neat and clean.

  As ridiculous as it may seem, some resumes do go out with smudges and coffee stains on them.
- Presented on quality paper with quality printing.

  Use the same paper stock on which your stationery is printed. If your copying machine won't deliver top-quality reproductions, it is worth the money to go to a good quick-print shop.
- Absolutely free of grammatical and typographical errors.

  Editing one's own writing is an extremely difficult task. Enlist someone else to edit and proofread your documents.
- Informative, concise and to the point.

  The one-page rule is arbitrary and restrictive. If you have important and interesting information to impart, go into a second page. It is unlikely that you have enough vital information to justify exceeding two pages. (An exception may be made if you choose to list references.)

Your resume should include these basic elements:
- Heading.

  Provide vital contact information: address, telephone and fax numbers.
- Summary of qualifications and/or the objective of your job search.

  You do not have to lay out your life's goals, but it is helpful to set out an overview of what you are all about.
- Educational background.

  List the school(s) from which you graduated and the years. There is controversy surrounding the question of whether or not to list your GPA. The answer depends on how good your grades were, and what sort of job you are looking for. If you are in the top quartile, list your GPA.

If you are going for a job in a technical field, such as engineering, this could be particularly important. Keep in mind, there are some companies where the first cut is made on the basis of grades. You can't change the facts if your grades are on the low side. It is probably better to leave out this data and wait for the subject to be raised in interviews. There are many times when the subject is not raised by candidate employers. This is more likely if your presentation is outstanding in all other regards.

- Experience.
  It is a good idea to review the earlier section on dynamic language and the ideas about making the most of your experience. Stress results, particularly those related even remotely to your career field.
- Activities, memberships, recognitions and honors.
  Don't be modest. List them all. Connections with your career field are, of course, important. So are other activities that recognize and validate leadership skills.
- References.
  The opinion is divided here. But it never hurts to list references, especially, if they include recognized names and positions. Remember, to always secure permission for the use of their names from those you list as references.

PREPARE THE OVERVIEW OF QUALIFICATIONS

The Overview of Qualifications is at the core of your campaign. This document is your communications platform from which you will develop your entire campaign. In some instances, you may use it in its entirety along with a sales letter personalized to fit a target employer. You may use the information from it as the heart of a stand-alone application letter. Or you may send the overview along with a letter and resume.

In any case, this document will serve two purposes. It will keep you on course through the various permutations of your sales materials. In addition, such a presentation will demonstrate your creativity and what Ray Holloway of International Paper Company refers to as "street smarts."

The five points in your overview should form a mosaic of logic that leaves no vital point unmade. The overall message should be loud and clear: HERE ARE FIVE PERSUASIVE REASONS YOU SHOULD HIRE ME.

Your five point presentation should answer the driving question on the mind of the buyer: What's in it for me? Avoid the point of view that most resumes take, if they express a point of view at all; that is "Here is what I want to do; my career objective is ..."

The first of your five sales points or reasons why you are the best choice for the job is a statement of objective in terms of the employer's interests. The next four points are intended to validate your ability to meet the stated objective.

The five points:

Objective:

(1) Who I am and what I can do for you.

Reasons I can reach this objective:

(2) Education.

(3) Experience.

(4) Extracurricular activities; honors/recognized leadership.

(5) Desire/attitude.

The document should be titled:

OVERVIEW
Qualifications Of
JOHN DOE
For A Position With
(NAME OF ORGANIZATION)

You will find it helpful as you begin to prepare this document to write out your presentation in narrative form. Don't worry about the format or the specifics of language at this point. Just let the flow go as you present your most persuasive case for why you should be employed by this organization. Recast it later to fit the suggested format of the document.

(You will find a sample of an Overview of Qualifications at the end of the book.)

CREATE SALES LETTERS

Think of sales letters as the catalysts. They are used to introduce you and to present your five selling points. The purpose of the letters is to trigger action by whetting interest in you as a potential asset for the employer. They must be attractive enough to command the attention of the reader and lead him into the other materials in your package. Remember the point of all of this is to convince the gatekeeper that you are worth the time, cost and effort of an interview.

The reality is that your letters, as well as your entire package of sales materials, must make their way through a very stiff weeding-out process.

In most instances, your initial sales letter will be your first and only opportunity to make a good first impression on the potential employer. This introductory letter will be awash in a sea of competing letters, all of which are clamoring for attention and an invitation to get in the front door.

All of your letters must represent class and quality in every respect. They must be well-written, brief and to the point. No one has time to figure out the points you are trying to make. Try never to exceed one page, no matter how fascinating and compelling you feel your selling messages are. The quality of your stationery must be first class. No errors in grammar or typing can be tolerated.

Address your letter to a real, live person – not an office, title or "to whom it may concern." The odds are it will never get past the first cut without such personalizing. If your research hasn't identified the proper recipient, go directly to the company for this vital information. Call the main switchboard, the human resources department or the department in which the job you want would be located. Don't hesitate to explain why you want the information.

Begin the process of creating your sales letter by composing a master document. This basic text can and should be customized for each candidate employer. This will not be difficult to accomplish if you are working with a computer. Never, never, never send out a form letter.

Take the time to do it right. Write, rewrite and rewrite this letter until it is compelling and convincing. You have no more than perhaps 225 words to get attention and convince the reader you are special, someone worth pursuing.

Your letter should be composed of three parts: *opening, selling message* and *closing*.

Opening

The opening paragraph is your headline. Its job is to compel the reader to read on. Try to hold it to no more than 40 words. Use the research you have conducted in identifying candidate employers. Relate to this particular employer by demonstrating that you are interested and resourceful enough to have developed knowledge about the organization. Explain that you are writing to ask for an interview in the conviction that you can demonstrate that your mutual interests will be served by your joining the organization.

Selling Message

Refer to your attached "five point" document. State positively that you believe this presentation demonstrates that the assets you possess can be put to work for the benefit of your employer and the long-term enhancement of your career.

The Closing

Use the closing to ask for the order. Clearly state that you are seeking an opportunity through an interview to discuss how your assets can be put to work for the employer. State a time (five to seven days out) when you will follow up by telephone to arrange an interview at a time and place convenient to the employer.

ASSURE TOTAL QUALITY

Arrange to have a third party (hopefully someone with strong talents in English composition, grammar and proofreading) edit your materials. This is very desirable even though you may be an expert grammarian and proofreader. It is difficult for most people to proof their own writing.

Keep two copies of your mailings. Place one in a master file of all correspondence. Put the other one in the file you have established for each candidate employer.

Timing is important. Schedule the mailing of your package so that it arrives on the potential employer's desk during the middle of the week. It is apt to get more attention then because Mondays are always hectic and many people are gone or pushing to close out the week on Fridays.

It is a good idea to run a quality control check on the materials you send out. Use this check list.

1. Is it logical and easily understood?
2. Is it persuasive?
3. Is it free of errors in grammar and typing?
4. Does the stationery convey a message of quality and professionalism?
4. What about the layout? Is it an easy and quick read?
5. Is the message expressed in terms of employer benefits?
6. Is the message expressed in dynamic, action-oriented words and terms?
7. Does the message include a call for action?

If you can't answer these questions in the positive, take time to make the necessary improvements before proceeding. Negatives in any one of these areas can be deal-killers.

(You will find examples of these several items for your sales package at the end of the book.)

MAKE THE MOST OF YOUR INTERVIEWS

Everything you have done up to this point – the setting of your goals, the analyzing of your assets, the creation of your marketing plan and the preparation of your sales materials – has been aimed at getting opportunities for face-to-face interviews so you can sell yourself in person.

In the normal course of events, the opportunities for job interviews come in two ways. The first and most likely is that as a result of your marketing campaign, you will be invited to visit the potential employer's offices. The second is that you will be able to line up interviews when recruiters visit your campus.

There is a third type of interview you should utilize. This is the one in which you visit with influentials in your chosen field or with leaders in the community to make contacts and gather information about your career prospects, the realities of working in the field you have selected and any leads for employment prospects.

You will use different tactics to secure the two different types of job interviews. But the way you prepare for and conduct yourself at these sessions should be basically the same. However, the "informational" interview requires a different approach.

INTERVIEWING FOR CONTACTS AND INFORMATION

Informational or contact interviews in which you visit with key people in your chosen field and with influentials in the community are crucial to your campaign to land that job you want and to make a success of it.

While you are not actually interviewing for a job on these occasions, it is inevitable that you will be assessed by the influential person with whom you are visiting. If you make a good impression, it is likely that you will have secured a good reference. And who knows, lightning may strike and you will get a job offer. If so, thank your lucky stars and chalk it up to serendipity.

The informational or contact interviews should serve three purposes for you.

(1) Provide valuable information about your career field and the market in general.

(2) Develop advice about your sales campaign and your approach to the job once you nail one down.

(3) Establish a valuable contact that may lead the way to other such connections.

Earlier, in the section dealing with networking with influentials, we addressed the matter of identifying and lining up these leaders for interviews. It is understandable that you might be reluctant to ask people at high levels to spend time discussing your future. But be reassured. As a recent graduate who is about the enter the world of work you have a particular advantage in getting in to see the influentials.

Remember, everyone likes to be asked to share his or her experiences and to give advice. So those you approach for help will be complimented and even flattered. Most of them can recall what it was like coming out of school, looking for that first job. Besides, most people in leadership positions want to identify talent for their organization or for their field of work.

Start at the top. Sure, it is more difficult to bag interviews with the chairman of the board than it is with the head of purchasing, for example. Yet look at the difference in potential payoffs. Anyway, if the person at or near the top can't see you, he can always refer your request to a subordinate. As you know, the reverse is not likely to happen.

If you are passed along to someone down the line, take the interview anyway. You don't want to be snobbish. Furthermore, you can never tell. Maybe you sparked some interest in the senior person and you are being checked out. In any case, the subordinate knows more than you know and can still be helpful.

If you strike out entirely, buck up your confidence and keep on working your list of leads.

Don't waste your time trying to line up an interview by telephone, unless a strong introduction has been made for you or you have a connecting link between another influential and the one you are trying to interview. In other words you need a name or contact who is important to the target you are pursuing.

A good letter is the ticket here.

Such a letter should be brief, to the point and respectful of the recipient's position vis a vis your needs. It should be specific as to what you want; that is, a few minutes of the person's time to gather information and advice about your career. The letter should include a promised action by you: that you will follow up with a telephone call on a given date to ask for a specific date for the interview. This initiative is necessary because you don't want to leave your request just hanging out there with the hope the busy person with whom you are seeking the interview will be so moved as to seek you out.

(An example of such a letter is provided at the end of this book.)

FOLLOW-UP CALLS ARE DIFFICULT, BUT NECESSARY

Follow-up calls are difficult, more so the higher up the ladder you are trying to make contact. But they must be made if you are going to benefit from interviews with the key people you are seeking.

Place your call quite early in the morning or very late in the afternoon before or after normal business hours. There is a slight chance the person you want to interview will answer the telephone. That would be splendid. Launch right in by identifying yourself and the purpose of your call. Recall your letter. Explain that you are launching your first career job search and would benefit greatly by an opportunity to share the interviewee's experience and knowledge. A generous dose of *honest* flattery never hurts.

However, odds are your call will be answered by the person's secretary. Explain that you are calling as promised to follow-up on your letter of such and such a date. State the purpose of your letter. Make it plain that you are a supplicant, just beginning your career, who is seeking insight and advice from Mr. or Mrs. Influential. Maintain your dignity but don't hesitate to throw yourself on the mercy of the court.

"I am very hopeful that he can see me for no more than 30 minutes at a time convenient to him," you declare. "Could you schedule an appointment for me?"

You most likely will be asked to leave your name and telephone number and wait for a callback. Hopefully, you will be given an explanation as to why the target person can't speak with you at the moment.

Be calm and patient. Express gratitude. Move on to the next task on your list of things to do. Wait two or three days. If you have not received a return call, try the above routine again. If you have not been able to get an appointment in three calls, mark that opportunity off your priority list.

CONDUCTING THE INFORMATIONAL INTERVIEW

The informational or contact interview is different in a major way from job interviews on or off campus. In this case, you are the interviewer. You are the one seeking information. It is your responsibility to ask the right questions and guide the discussion at least until you have sparked enough interest on the part of the interviewee that he or she takes over.

Make certain you have done your research on the person you are interviewing. Know what they do and what they have done. Let them know that you know. Compliments and respect are the order of the day.

Whatever you do, don't go into such a session without a strategy as to what you want to learn and how you are going to get the information. You would be out on strike one if you were foolish enough to begin by saying, "I don't know what I want to do. Can you help me?"

Begin by clearly stating your objective for the meeting. Be absolutely sincere and serious. You are using up valuable time that won't come your way again. You want to benefit from the interviewee's experience and knowledge about either a specific career field or about a career objective. You want to learn about the employment market in general. You want to ask that person to share insight into what it takes to succeed.

Define your objective for your first job. Review the five points that are the key to your sales presentation. It would be very advantageous if the interviewee would take the time to read your Overview of Qualifications. You can judge by the atmosphere and the tempo of the meeting as to whether it is wise to share the document at this point. Whatever happens, try to review the five points and get a feedback.

SUGGESTED POINTS FOR DISCUSSION

You must be flexible, ready to let the interviewee range about from subject to subject if that is the person's preferred style. However, be sure to cover most of the points that follow before the session is concluded.

(1) What are the major ingredients of success in the chosen industry or profession?

(2) What are the good points and what are the bad points about the chosen career field?

(3) How has the field changed in the last 10 years?

(4) What is the outlook for jobs now and growth in the future?

(5) What have been the highlights of the interviewee's career?

(6) How do your interview skills and education stack up against competition and requirements in this field?

(7) What advice would the interviewee offer?

(8) Suggestions for other such informational interviews?

You asked for no more than 30 minutes. Be mindful of the clock. Don't be surprised if the interviewee goes on beyond the scheduled time. He may be finding this session the most productive and relaxing period of the day. Take the time you can get, but don't overstay your welcome.

Leave with a sincere expression of appreciation. Depending on how the discussion went, you may want to ask for permission to make another contact.

FOLLOW UP FOR SURE

You have made a contact that is potentially worth gold in your career bank. Nurture it with a swift and effective follow-up letter. Express appreciation for the time and sharing of knowledge and experience. Outline any actions you will take as a result of the meeting such as making other contacts, changing your presentation and the like.

INTERVIEWS IN THE CANDIDATE EMPLOYER'S OFFICE

Let's take a look at the most likely scenario as far as actual job interviews are concerned.

The telephone rings. It's the good news you have been waiting for. You have been invited to come in for the first interview with one of your candidate companies.

You should approach this opportunity with the clear, sobering recognition that the first interview is the most important step in the hiring process.

Unless you have ice water in your veins instead of blood, you will be nervous. You are approaching crunch time.

Keep these things in mind as you prepare for the meeting:
(1) You would not have been invited for the interview if the organization did not have a need.
(2) You would not have been invited for the interview if the organization had not felt you showed enough promise to justify their investment of time and money to look you over.
(3) This will not be your only opportunity.
(4) You, not the interviewer, control your destiny.

It will help you keep things in perspective if you look at this situation from the interviewer's viewpoint. This person who is seeking to fill a position will be making a high-risk decision. The employer will be making a considerable investment of time and money in you or whoever is hired. The question is, what will be the return on the organization's investment in the person chosen for the job? The decision is being viewed in terms of a relationship that hopefully will last over several years. During the initial period, the new employee will not be running at full speed. In fact, the interviewer is looking at candidates in terms of the third and fourth positions they will hold, not just the starting spot. So, you are not the only one at the interview who is under pressure.

Up to now, all the potential employer knows about you comes from the sales material you provided, and, perhaps, by word-of-mouth comments from those who know you. But again that has been good enough to get you in the front door.

HUMAN DIMENSIONS TAKE OVER

Now you have the opportunity to put human dimensions on the product the recruiter is evaluating. This is where style, personality, interpersonal and communications skills and that catchall term, "chemistry," come in to play. The fact is, in most cases, it is the personal, human qualities that make the big difference in the final decision. *People hire people they identify with, like and trust.*

Never forget, there is a great deal of equality on the market in terms of education and experience. You have been successful in making your qualifications stand out from the crowd. Otherwise, you would not have gotten this far in the process. You can assume you have cleared the hurdle of basic qualifications, which can be more or less judged *quantitatively:* college attended, grades, experience, ability to communicate in writing, demonstrated leadership and the like. The potential employer believes you have the basic education and skills for the job. Now, you are into the area of *qualitative* values. The driving questions from this point forward are more apt to be about how you will fit in the organization, your ability to communicate and get things done through others, your ambition and character.

An interview is essentially a weeding-out process. The interviewer has had an opportunity to review a lot of materials from many candidates in one form or another. Presumably, the majority of the applicants have been eliminated on the basis of their resumes. Now the organization is looking at the survivors, all but one or a few of whom must be eventually cut out. So while the interviewing process is looking for positives, it is essentially a negative exercise to be survived.

Stop for a minute and consider the central issue that exists between the interviewer and the interviewee. Both are asking the same question: "What's in it for me?"

The interviewer is asking himself these and many more challenging questions:

"I have to fill this job (or jobs) within a given time. What can this person do for me? If I make a good selection, it will be to my credit. If I make a mistake, it will count against me. Can this person cut it? Will he fit into the organization? What about work habits? Am I getting facts here or is this candidate's fiction? Is there a better candidate out there somewhere?"

At the same time the interviewee is wondering:

"Am I getting a true picture or is this person trying to sell me a bill of goods? Are these promises real? What kind of place would this be to work? What about living in this area? Can I get a better offer?"

In every hiring process both parties finally have to take a leap of faith based on intuition or "gut" feelings generated by visceral impressions and senses.

Think of the interview as a learning process. While interviewers are taking your measure, you also will have the opportunity to size up the organization as a potential employer. While a one-on-one visit with a representative of the organization is not all-revealing, it certainly can give you some sense about the pace and environment of the organization.

Also, you will have an opportunity to learn more about the interviewing process and your skills, or lack of them, in making the most of such opportunities.

INTERVIEWING IS A TWO-WAY PROCESS

Remember that interviewing is like any other communication process. It is two-way: sending and receiving messages. To our detriment, most of us spend too much time on the former and too little on the latter.

Here are five tips that will help you improve your listening skills:

1. Be aware always that waiting your turn to speak is not listening.
2. Focus like a laser beam on what the interviewer is saying. Listen to the words and the spaces of silence. Both say a lot.
3. Assure the interviewer you are interested and you are listening by maintaining eye contact, nodding your head, offering an occasional "I see," "I understand," and the like.
4. Concentrate on the facts. Collect them carefully, both from the words and the silences, as they are presented. Take notes. Don't let yourself get diverted by trying to analyze what you hear on the spot. You can interpret all of this information later.
5. Don't get sidetracked by the interviewer's personal appearance or mannerisms. Overlook any biased or irritating statements.

Communications involve not only verbal messages. Nonverbal actions speak louder than words. The way you stand, sit, gesture, frown and smile speak volumes. Experts say that at least 65 percent of all communications are nonverbal.

For instance, what message do you telegraph if you are slumped back in your chair as compared with sitting erect, leaning slightly forward as if concentrating on every word spoken to you? Consider

71

the difference between the messages you transmit when your shoulders are erect versus when you are slumped over. Or what are you "saying" when your arms are folded rigidly across your chest rather than held loosely at your side and involved in gesturing to underscore your key points?

BE PREPARED FOR THE INTERVIEW

Planning and preparation for the actual interview are everything at this point.

First of all, be aware of the six criteria on which you will be rated in most interviews. These will be applied by the interviewer filling out a rating form or referencing his impressions against a mental checklist. Your rating may eventually be fed into a computer for a totally impersonal rating.

The key criteria include:

(1) Personal impression you make.

　　Neatness in personal appearance; self-confidence and maturity.

(2) Preparation for interview.

　　Knowledge of potential employer; organized preparation; intelligent questions.

(3) Communications skills.

　　Written materials and oral skills.

(4) Attitude.

　　Enthusiasm, sincerity and interest.

(5) Competence.

　　Education, experience, and demonstrated leadership abilities.

(6) Chemistry.

　　Suitability and "fit" with culture of potential employer's organization.

Make an effort to learn about the kind of interviews the company usually conducts. Get a fix on the people who will be conducting the interview. This is a tough assignment. You may not be able to develop much here. Go ahead, try anyway. Seek out others who have been interviewed by the company. Talk to people who do business with the organization.

Are their interviews formal or informal? Do they administer aptitude and other kinds of tests? Are the interviews deliberately stressful? What about "tricky" questions? How long do the sessions last? Are you likely to see more than one person?

Try to get a feel for the environment. It will have a lot to do with your dress for the interview and how you approach the occasion in general. For example, you could anticipate a different mode of dress and general atmosphere in a bank as compared with a computer company in Silicon Valley.

It will help also to do a little negative thinking. What could bomb your chances?

1. Being late for the appointment.
2. Making a negative physical appearance in dress, neatness and posture; reflecting low energy or a lackadaisical attitude.
3. Being too informal and familiar; trying to be humorous.
4. Letting attention and eye contact wander.
5. Being indifferent or negative.
6. Dropping names and being the "big shot."
7. Being unprepared and unresponsive.
8. Exhibiting too much interest in the benefits (i.e. compensation, vacations, etc.)
9. Talking too much; constantly interrupting; not listening.
10. Evasiveness; unable to explain voids in your file.
11. Being critical of past work experiences or teachers.
12. Failure to ask intelligent questions about the job.
13. Being overconfident or underconfident.

DEMONSTRATE YOUR INTEREST IN THE JOB

Demonstrate your interest in the job. This may seem like strange and unnecessary advice. But too often, job candidates foolishly overestimate their positions vis a vis the market and think it is a good idea to play hard to get.

The rule is you are selling, they are buying.

Your going-in strategy should be to communicate to the interviewer that you have made a studied effort to learn a great deal about the organization. There is absolutely nothing you can do that will make a better impression. The fact that you have expended the effort to gather such information shows interest, a proactive nature, intelligence and seriousness. You have already demonstrated as much in your sales literature and it is probably one of the reasons you have made it this far. Now reinforce that favorable impression with updated information.

You have done the homework. Go back to the file you have assembled on the appropriate industry, the company being interviewed and the locale.

Absorb that information so that it can be readily called up. Make a list of the points you think you can make to the best advantage.

Now refer once again to your Overview of Qualifications and your other sales literature. Burn those five vital reasons you should be hired into your mind, so that you will be ready to drive them home during the interview.

SET YOUR STRATEGY

Think through your communications strategy. You should have a general scenario in mind in which you make these five points at least three times. Put it in outline form. A good way to think about this is to go to the well-established guideline for making a speech: tell them what you are going to tell them, tell them and tell them what you told them.

This means making your five points in an opening statement; bringing them up again during the course of the interview; and getting them out a third time in the summary you will make.

It is up to you, not the interviewer, to bring out all of the reasons you should be hired and fit them into a smooth, easily understood mosaic.

Visualize the day of the interview from the time you get up in the morning until you leave the site of the interview. See yourself scoring on every point. Your physical image is strong and positive. Your communications skills are running along full throttle. The vibes between you and the interviewer are great. Repeat this positive visualization process every day from the moment of invitation until you leave the potential employer's offices with a sincere "thank you" to the receptionist and the parking lot attendant.

Rehearse the interview. Get before a mirror, hopefully a full-length one, and practice your physical presentation. Look at yourself greeting the receptionist, introducing yourself to the interviewer's secretary and finally to the person himself. Practice your opening statement over and over again.

Recruit a friend, hopefully someone who has been through the process, to act as an interviewer to put you through the paces. Be sure that plenty of tough questions are included in these rehearsals.

When you are satisfied, get someone to videotape your presentation and the "Q&A" session.

Repeat to yourself over and over again: "I will be relaxed, but I will not let my guard down for one minute until I am well away from the interview."

Realize that just because the interviewer closes his notebook and puts his pencil away the interview is not over. In fact, some interviewers will use this as a ploy to get the interviewee to let his guard down and reveal too much. The same applies to discussions at lunch or dinner. The *real interview* may be just beginning when it appears to be ending.

It is a good rule to remember the story of Fred Astaire, the great dancer. One of his partners said that he always told her before they began to film a sequence, "Relax, my dear, but don't make any mistakes."

THE DAY OF THE INTERVIEW

It is I-Day!

Hopefully, you have had a good night's rest. The night before an interview is no time to go partying with the old crowd. Relax. Your nervousness is appropriate, even helpful if you don't go off the deep end.

Enjoy a good, bland breakfast. Dress for the occasion in a wardrobe you have already selected and made sure to have clean and pressed. Be sure your shoes are well shined.

Review the list of vital information you have already assembled. It should include clear directions on how to get from your home to the interview site; a list of telephone numbers of the person or persons you will be dealing with this day; your file on the company; the outline of your opening statement including the five vital points.

Pack your briefcase with the above information and your interview supplies. (You may feel that a briefcase is a bit ostentatious and it could be in some situations. But in most instances it will be to your benefit to carry a briefcase as it will allow you to organize your materials and signal a businesslike approach.) Include several pencils or pens, along with a notebook. Also, pack the morning newspaper or a current news or business magazine.

Leave home in a clean car, allowing plenty of time to get to the interview site with some time to spare. You cannot afford to arrive at the last minute with no time to compose yourself, freshen up and get a feel for the place. Ten minutes on site is usually about right. If you encounter delays and see that you are going to be late, call the interviewer's secretary or assistant (whose number you should have in your file) to explain and apologize for your delay. Don't call the interviewer personally unless absolutely necessary.

Upon arrival, find a restroom whether or not you need "to go." Make sure you are looking your best. You don't want to go through the interview wondering if your hair is straight and you are properly buttoned up.

The interview begins the minute you arrive on the site. Exhibit a friendly, but somewhat restrained presence. In other words, be nice, but not too familiar. Conduct yourself in an appropriate manner with *everyone* you encounter. (The guard at the parking lot may be the son of the person interviewing you.) Unless invited to do otherwise, never use first names or flippant greetings. Make it Mr., Mrs. or Miss. Recognize an important fact of organizational life for now and later: receptionists and secretaries can make you or break you. They are the gatekeepers. They always have the opportunity to pass positive or negative comments to their bosses and others. They can expedite or block your seeing the decision makers. They can even let you know the mood in the office of their boss.

KEEP COOL

After you have announced yourself, don't be surprised if you are kept waiting for some time. Do not show disappointment or impatience. It is a good idea to ask the person who received you if there is any current company literature available for reading, such as an annual or interim report, an employee magazine or sales literature. There may be other reading material in the waiting room. Given a choice, pick up *The Wall Street Journal* or *Business Week,* rather than *People* magazine. If nothing is available go to a seat and pull out the reading materials you brought along. Review your communications strategy.

Be alert to your nonverbal communications. Sit back, relaxed in your chair. Do not twist and squirm while seated. Never pace.

If the delay is running unduly long, say 45 minutes, ask to use a telephone, explaining you have to rearrange another appointment. If you don't have another appointment, call your home number. This little pretense won't hurt anyone and it is a subtle way to communicate that you are in demand and to remind the receptionist that you are still there waiting.

THE FORMAL INTERVIEW BEGINS

You are finally ushered in to meet the interviewer, the person who holds the keys to the second gate that will admit you for more interviews and finally an offer.

Think of the meeting as a discussion about your future.

You want the offer of a job. The interviewer wants you to fill the need.

The importance of the initial five minutes of the first interview cannot be overemphasized. As already noted, this is the only chance you will have to make a good first impression. Give it your best shot.

A dry, firm handshake, a direct unwavering look in the eye, and an erect bearing will set the stage in your favor from the very beginning. No matter how tired you are of hearing your sales messages or how nervous you may be, you have to appear fresh, enthusiastic and confident.

Wait for your host to invite you to be seated. If he takes a seat behind his desk and invites you to be seated across from him you know it is likely to be a more formal proceeding. If, on the other hand, he comes around his desk to sit facing you in a side chair you can expect a somewhat informal interview. In any case, you can not afford to forget your mission and the businesslike way you must conduct yourself.

Sit tight. Resist the impulse to start talking. Wait until the interviewer makes an opening statement or asks the first question. Maintain eye contact if he is looking you over. This period may seem like an eternity. If he is shuffling papers in preparation for the discussion, relieve the tensions by taking the occasion to retrieve your notebook out of your briefcase and preparing yourself to take extensive notes.

It is a delicate task, but you must take control of the interview as soon as possible. You want to take this high ground without being overly aggressive or showing disrespect for the dynamics of the relationship.

You can begin to achieve control after the interviewer has opened the discussion by expressing appreciation for the opportunity provided. Move quickly into your opening statement. This is your opportunity to say something to this effect:

"I have looked forward to this meeting. My research shows that Acme Gizmos is a company I would like to work for. After all it is not every company that has the growth record in sales and earnings that Acme has demonstrated. I am also very excited about the recent acquisitions I have been reading about. Before we have finished our meeting I would like to know more about your recent move into laser-based gizmos."

Now shift gears.

"I studied a lot of literature about the company and I have some feel for your needs, but I think I could do a better job for you in responding to your questions," you can say, "if you would tell me more about the position I am being interviewed for."

You can do a quick assessment of how your assets fit the bill. You may want to refine or refocus your presentation based on what you hear.

Hopefully, at this point you can move on to an opening summary of your case. This should be based on your "five reasons why" document. These are the vital points you have determined to make to show why you are the logical choice.

Once again, you and the potential employer share a mutual interest that revolves around a question on the minds of both parties: What's in it for me?

IT'S TIME FOR THE Q&A

Now is the time for questions and answers by both parties. Most people assume the interviewing process is an occasion for the potential employer to do most of the asking. Do not approach the interview with that attitude. You are there to answer questions, of course, but you are also there to ask questions.

You will get both positive and negative questions. Most will be designed to draw you out, to measure your communications skills, or to clear up any confusion. Some will be deliberately stressful. Some may be downright "tricky." You may also get some that are illegal or in poor taste.

Each type of question requires a response strategy of its own. In any case, take your time to think through your answers before speaking. Keep your five vital points in mind and try to relate your answers to them.

The positive questions, those seeking information and clarifying points, are the easy ones. You know your information hands down; articulate it in a forthright manner.

Keep your cool with the stressful and "tricky" ones. Take the facts as they are and make your best effort to turn these curve balls into home runs. For example, suppose the interviewer says:

"If I have read your background correctly, you dropped out of school for what would normally have been the first semester of your sophomore year. What was that all about?"

Your positive response could be:

"I am very glad you brought that up. I was going to mention that. By the end of my freshman year I was thoroughly confused about what I wanted to do. I had thought I wanted to go to medical school. My grandfather was a doctor. But I just wasn't happy, and frankly my grades – particularly in the sciences – were not satisfactory.

"I decided I was wasting my time and my parents' money going to college until I established my career goals. So I took a job that summer and worked through the fall while I sorted things out. It was the best thing I could have done. I read a lot and talked to many people about careers. I decided I wanted to major in business. I got focused.

"I returned to school at midterm and knuckled down to work. My grades show the result. Where I was just barely passing before, when I came back to school I began scoring at the 3.0 to 4.0 level. In addition, I got involved in a number of very positive activities on campus."

You are not likely to get illegal questions or those in poor taste at this point. These might include questions about your religion, sex life, marital status, organizational affiliations and the like. If you are put in this kind of situation, be direct, firm and polite in your response. Control yourself and the situation. Try to turn this negative time into a positive.

Depending on the question, you might respond by saying:

"Could you please explain how that issue bears on the opportunity we are discussing?"

"I don't think we should be discussing that question."

"That does not seem to be an appropriate question."

Do not compromise if such a line of questioning persists.

If this honest and legitimate response to an illegitimate question penalizes your chances for getting the job, so be it. If the interviewer, and by extension the organization, condones this sort of thing you probably would not be happy working there anyway.

TYPICAL QUESTIONS; SUGGESTED ANSWERS

Here are some questions that you may encounter and ideas about how to respond to them. Of course, whatever questions come up you will have to frame your own answers based on the *facts*. The interviewer will know full well that you are going to put the best "spin" possible on the answers. He will not be surprised if you skip over the rough spots. In all cases, stick to the basic truth.

Always, repeat always, put your answers to his questions – in fact all of your communications – in terms of the potential employer's interests.

Why do you want this job?

You have already indicated your answer in your opening statement. Take this as another opportunity to display your interest in and knowledge about the company. Speak to the company's record of growth, its policies and how it fits your ambitious nature.

Why should this organization hire you?

Here's an opportunity to restate your five vital points. You can summarize it by saying, "I am convinced that given the opportunity I can do a good job in terms of hard results and make you glad you hired me."

What salary do you expect?

It is too early to have an intelligent response. You are more interested in knowing what the opportunities are and how this job fits into the organization.

What are your greatest strengths?

Don't be modest. Go to your five reasons why you should be selected. Relate them to the needs of the company whenever you can.

What are your greatest weaknesses?

We all have them. Be honest, but pick weaknesses that can be seen as strengths. These include: impatience; being too serious about work and life in general; being too demanding of self and associates; or getting so absorbed in the problem of the moment.

What have been your one or two biggest mistakes or failures?

Again, try to select mistakes or failures that resulted despite your best efforts. Ran for class president and lost by three votes. Started a business in college and saw it fail because of lack of capital.

(Note: Most interviewers really do not expect to elicit meaningful facts with these sorts of negative questions. They are more interested in the emotional reactions they get. Nonverbal communication is especially important at these points.)

What would you like to improve about yourself?

Relate your answer to things that would strengthen your performance on the job you are interviewing for and higher ones. Include a statement of a more general nature such as acquire a better understanding of economics.

How would your friends and associates describe you?

That is a tough one. You hope they see you as honest, fair and hard working. You would feel comfortable in letting them speak for you.

What motivates you?

The same things that motivate all ambitious people. Responsibility, respect, opportunities to grow and money.

What do you do in your spare time?

Be honest. Hopefully, you can honestly report that you have some spare-time interests related to your career or to public service.

What do you read?

You don't have to be specific, but if you have been following the strategies outlined in this book you have been reading materials that relate to the company and its industry. You can say finishing school didn't leave you much time for reading anything other than academic literature. However, more recently you have been studying business publications, particularly those pertinent to this opportunity. Mention specific trade journals. Name your daily newspaper and news magazines. When time permits, you would like to get back to reading American history (or politics, current fiction, etc.)

What are your long-term goals?

You want to concentrate on the immediate goal of getting this job and making a success of it. You plan to continue to develop your qualifications by going to night school and taking courses. You would like to move up in the organization in a logical fashion. Frankly, you would like some day to be a senior officer of the corporation.

If you are employed you would hope to work with the appropriate people to develop a career path plan with specific objectives.

What do you like to do/do not like to do?

Of course, there are things on both sides of the equation. You know there is always the bitter with the sweet. You have demonstrated you do what it takes to get the job done.

Do you mind working for someone of the opposite sex?

No. It is the job and the opportunities it represents that count.

How do you handle criticism?

Everyone has some problem with accepting criticism. But you have learned there is almost always a better way to do things and someone who can tell you about it. You don't particularly like to be in a position where criticism is deserved, but you can take it in stride as a part of life.

You seem rather aggressive. Are you?

You hope you are aggressive within reason. You are focused on your goals and those of the organization. You push for them, but you are no Attila The Hun.

How would you feel about firing someone?

You wouldn't like it, no one does. But you would if the circumstances dictated it and if proper procedures had been followed.

What will you do if you don't get this job?

Of course, you will be disappointed. You will be the loser and, frankly, you think the organization will be the loser, too. However, you have other opportunities and will continue pursuing them.

Did you do as well as you could have in school?

Frankly, no. But does anyone? Any one of us can always do better. But you feel well prepared for the job being discussed. (If you were a "straight A" student, say you could have been involved in more extracurricular activities or taken more advanced courses.)

Do you ever lose your temper?

Of course, you do. Everyone who has any spunk does. Some degree of temper is healthy, so long as it doesn't get out of control. You try to keep yours under control.

What causes you to lose your temper?

You get out of sorts with people who don't meet deadlines as promised. You also can get mad when people are being treated unfairly and when you are treated as if you were a fool.

Here are examples of other questions you might encounter.

What do you really want to do with your life?

Why did you choose your career field?

How would you describe yourself?

What do you think it will take to be successful in this organization?

Can you describe what you would consider to be an ideal relationship between you and your bosses?

What would be your ideal job?

QUESTIONS YOU SHOULD ASK

There are a number of questions that you should ask during the interview. You demonstrate your interest and seriousness when you ask pertinent questions. If you fail to ask questions you come off as uninformed, timid or without interest in getting the job.

You can ask your questions as opportunities arise during the course of the interview, or you can save them until the end of the session.

In any case, here are some examples of the kinds of questions you should pose.

Is there a formal description for the job we are discussing?

Where is the job located?

To whom would I report?

Is this a new position or would I be replacing someone?

If this is a replacement, why did the other person leave?

In this case, how long has the job been open?

How many people have held this job in the past?

Is this a permanent position in the company?

Are you interviewing other candidates?

What are the prospects for advancement?

What are the downside risks associated with this job?

Is there a continuing education and management development program with career paths in place?

How would my performance be measured? Is a formal evaluation program in place?

Would I be permitted/encouraged to take part in public service activities?

How soon do you expect to make a decision?

What are the next steps?

Go back to that section of your marketing plan where you defined the kind of organization you want to work for as a source for additional questions.

CLOSING THE MEETING

The interview has been going on for some time now. You have had plenty of opportunity to get your sales message across. Be very sensitive to the signals you are getting from the interviewer. Is he beginning to look at his watch or fidget in his chair? Is it time to bring the session to a close? Better you leave on your own volition than be invited to leave. Besides, it is a good idea to follow the old show business adage: always leave them wanting more.

It is time to summarize. You have told the interviewer what you were going to tell him and then you told him. Now, by way of summary, tell him what you have told him.

Leave no doubt that you are interested in the opportunity. You want an invitation to come back for one or more additional interviews at the very least.

"Mr. Johnson, I really like all that I have heard here today," you can say to begin your summary. "I want to work for Gizmos. I have tried to make five vital points here today as to why you should hire me. Let me restate them."

Hand a printed copy of the five reasons why you should be hired to the interviewer. Explain you want to provide him with an easy reference to the reasons you are right for the job.

Ask for some explanation of the next steps and the timing in the selection process.

Conclude by asking if there is any more information you can supply or any steps you can take to advance the process. Express interest in meeting other people in the organization. Depending on what transpires at this point, ask if you may call on the fifth working day. Get the name of the person you should call.

Leave with a firm handshake and a sincere "thank you for your time."

Don't forget to thank the secretary and receptionists, anyone you came in contact with during your visit. Check with these valuable sources to be sure you have the proper names and titles of everyone with whom you had contact.

HANDLING MORE INTERVIEWS

Many times the primary interviewer will want candidates to interview with others in the organization. Certainly, this is a good sign if it happens in your interview. You passed the first test. At the very least you know they are following a thorough process. Do not let your guard down. When you are handed off to the next interviewer, rev up your energy and repeat the strategy you used in the first visit. The two or more interviewers will compare notes.

Or you may be invited to go to lunch or dinner with one or more interviewers. Obviously, this is also good news, but there are pitfalls to be avoided. After a thorough going over in the interview(s) that have preceded the invitation to visit in a more relaxed setting, the tendency is to breathe a sigh of relief that you've gotten that trial over with. You may even be picking up signals that lead you to think you have the job in the bag when the interviewers use such phrase as

"When you start to work…" or "You will find this to be a good place to work." Don't assume anything. The chase is still on.

You may indeed have it going your way at this point, but it would be an extremely unusual situation if a final decision were made that quickly.

If you go out for a meal, be friendly, let your personality come through a bit more relaxed, but be vigilant. Interviews over a meal can be extremely stressful, just as they can be a great opportunity. There probably won't be any notepads in view, but the notetaking goes on. (Have handy-size file cards on which you can unobtrusively jot notes. Be aware that excessive notetaking over lunch may be seen as bad form. In fact, it is forbidden in some private luncheon clubs.)

You are there to sell your product, not to celebrate. You may be tired of your five vital points, but keep working them into conversation.

Don't order a drink containing alcohol even if your host and others are going to have one. Order food that is easy and neat to eat. Corn on the cob and fried chicken are out. Neither do you want to contend with tomato sauce from your pasta running down your chin. Avoid the most expensive and the least expensive items.

You will have had time to reflect on what you heard and saw in the morning. Use that knowledge to ask questions to get more information and to demonstrate you were paying attention. Be sure you make a note of the proper names and titles of all persons present or with whom you came in contact prior to lunch.

By the way, you can pick up some important clues as to what kind of organization you are interviewing by the way the interviewers conduct the extended session.

When your host indicates the meal time is about over, use the same closing tactics as suggested above. Yes, it is appropriate to repeat the points about your interest, follow-up calls, etc.

FOLLOWING UP

Take the first opportunity you have after leaving the interviews to review and enlarge on your notes. Put your first impressions of the people and the situations on paper. The form that follows will be helpful in this regard. Fill out such a form for each interview or visit with each candidate employer.

This will prove to be a valuable document for reference in your later discussions. This document will also be an interesting and helpful point of reference if you go to work with this organization.

INTERVIEW RECORD

Name of Organization: _____

Place of Interview: _____

Person(s) Interviewing: _____

_____

Information Developed About The Organization: _____

_____

_____

_____

Information Developed About The Job: _____

_____

_____

_____

Next Steps: _____

_____

_____

_____

Impressions of People and Organization: _____

_____

_____

_____

Key Questions Asked: _____

_____

_____

_____

Revisions of Answers:* _____

_____

_____

_____

Changes In Presentation/Strategy: _____

_____

_____

_____

Other Observations: _____

_____

_____

_____

_____

_____

_____

_____

_____

_____

_____

_____

_____

_____

*If after more thought, you conclude you should have answered in a different way, record your revised answers for use in the future.

Send letters no later than the next day to the principals with whom you came in contact, including the primary interviewer's secretary. Thank them for their time and courtesies. Make a note of any special consideration, especially with the secretary.

Your letter to the primary interviewer should restate your interest in the job and reflect some new information or insight you gained. Yes, use your five vital points yet one more time. Refer to what you consider to have been the key points covered during the discussions. If lunch was involved, make mention of the fact that it was an enjoyable occasion; it was a welcomed opportunity to get better acquainted with some of the people you hope to be working with. Be sure to follow up on unanswered questions or information requested. Set a date on which you will telephone him.

Your letters to other interviewers should be personalized according to your discussions.

TELEPHONE CALLS ARE VITAL

Follow-up telephone calls can be difficult and frustrating, but they are extremely important.

The fact is the candidate employer is not sitting on pins and needles waiting for your call.

But you have promised to call back on the fifth business day. Do it without fail. Place your call directly to the lead interviewer. If that person is out of town or otherwise unavailable, ask to speak with his secretary or the receptionist. Explain your purpose and determine when the interviewer will be available or get the name of some other person with whom you can speak. (Hopefully, you will have made a note of other persons with whom you can make a productive telephone contact.)

Let's assume you are able to reach the primary interviewer, who is quarterbacking the process. You have a few minutes at most; take full advantage of the time.

"Hello, Mr. Jones. This is John Doe. I had the opportunity to interview with you on (the exact date). As promised, I am following up on our meeting. I have thought a lot about our conversation and I believe more strongly than ever that I could make a real contribution to Acme Gizmos' program.

"Mr. Jones, I want to come to work for Gizmos. I believe I can deliver a good return on your investment in me."

Pause. Give Mr. Jones a chance to respond.

Chances are he will say that no decision has been made as yet.

Ask if you are one of the leading candidates. If the answer is "yes," express appreciation and ask, "Can you share with me what the next steps are and what timetable you have in mind?"

If the interviewer says you are not a candidate, tell him it would be very helpful to know where you fell short and ask for suggestions for improving your presentation. In any case, express appreciation for the opportunity to interview and ask that your expression of interest be maintained in their active files.

In either case, fire off a follow-up letter. You either are excited to know you are a leading candidate and you will proceed as you were advised. Or you express regret that there was not a fit between you and the organization. Ask that you be kept in mind for other opportunities.

INTERVIEWING ON CAMPUS

Experience shows you are less likely to interview on campus than on the candidate employer's home base. Most employers do not visit campuses. They simply are not prepared to handle this type of recruiting, or it is not cost effective for their limited needs.

On-campus recruiting is particularly suited for special fields, such as engineering and accounting. Opportunities for interviewing while you are still on campus may not apply immediately and specifically to your interests.

However, you cannot afford to ignore recruiters who visit your college. You may strike gold in one of these sessions, particularly if you are in the top quartile of your graduating class. At the very least, interviewing on campus can provide you with valuable experience in this art. Good recruiters can generally spot those who have had some experience with interviewing. They like that in candidates because it makes their interviewing more productive and it shows initiative on the part of the interviewee.

Your college's placement office is the gatekeeper for your successful use of on-campus interviews. If you have followed the strategies outlined in this book, you will have established a good working relationship with the staff of the placement office before you get into your senior year.

As the recruiting season approaches, advise the appropriate person in the placement office that you would like to avail yourself of any interviewing opportunities that fit your career objectives. Make sure the placement staff has your sales package on file, including your five reasons overview document and any other materials you feel will contribute to rounding out the picture of your assets.

When you get a list of the names and dates of visiting recruiters, identify those in which you have an interest. If there are none or not enough of top interest to fill up your "dance card," select one or two additional ones where there are near-fits. You never know when lightning may strike. Moreover, every interview increases your experience, your abilities and your confidence. Hopefully, one or more of those "wild cards" will make you a stronger candidate for the job you want.

Check with the placement office. If they have no objections to your doing so, dispatch a sales letter with your "five reasons" to the recruiter who will be visiting your campus. Declare that you are looking forward to interviewing with him on such and such a date to discuss how your assets can be put to work for his organization.

There may be a social event of some kind in connection with the recruiters' visits. By all means attend such a function. Meet every recruiter you can. Recruiter A may be looking for engineers and you are a marketing major. But when A gets back to the office he will be talking with his associates, B and C, who are searching for candidates in other fields. If you make a good enough impression, A may pass your name to B or C.

Look your best. Act your best. Hand out your "business card." Make a point of reminding those recruiters with whom you have scheduled an interview that you are looking forward to your discussions.

Follow the same tactics as suggested earlier for the interviews in candidate employers' offices.

CHOOSE YOUR JOB

Finally, you have one or more real live job offers in hand. While you were struggling with your search and experiencing the roller coaster period ranging from elation and high hopes to worry and nervousness, it was hard to imagine that this time would come. But you have done a good and thorough job with your campaign and you are within sight of the goal line.

But hold up. Don't uncork the celebratory bottle of champagne just yet. Unfortunately, an offer does not always mean a done deal. Don't stop your search until you have a firm commitment – signed, sealed and delivered – saying that you have a job under terms that are acceptable to you.

Unfortunately, organizations, even the most powerful, are not always able to follow through on offers. Market conditions change. Hiring freezes are imposed. Organizations get turned upside down.

So keep a firm grasp on all of your offers and prospects until you are safely on someone's payroll.

When one or more offers are received, take your time. Be thorough in your evaluation.

While you must be careful and deliberate in making your decision, do not let too much time elapse before you respond to the offers. Treat *all offers* with respect wherever they fall on your list of preferences. Respond to each and every one in a positive and enthusiastic fashion.

You don't want to blow what you have worked so long and hard to get. Use the 24-hour rule. If you have the slightest doubt about accepting an offer, you should feel comfortable in asking for 24 hours to think it over. Of course, you want to indicate your strong interest when you ask for more time.

No offer will be perfect, but if one clearly tops all others, don't dally. Accept it quickly and with enthusiasm. Don't get clever and try to squeeze a little more out of the orange. The same applies if you have run an exhaustive campaign and you have only one offer, which is within the range of acceptability, and no others are in sight.

If you have several offers that you want to mull over, respond to each organization you are considering. Express your appreciation and serious interests. Say that you are evaluating other opportunities, including this one, and that you need a specific period of time to complete the process. Unless you have in hand all of the information you need to compare offers and make a decision, request an opportunity to come in for another visit.

There is no denying if you do have an offer you are running some risk if you do not accept it immediately. You can tell a great deal about an organization by its reaction to a legitimate request for a bit of breathing room. Recruiters are under pressure, too. They don't have a great deal of time to fiddle faddle. But impatience or a worse reaction to your request for time is a red flag that should not go unnoticed.

The good news is that most organizations will understand that you are facing a big decision – just as they are – and that it is proper and reasonable to want a bit of time to decide.

THERE ARE NO ROSES WITHOUT THORNS

No job is perfect. There are positive and negative aspects to every situation. Consider each position you are evaluating in its entirety. Can you live with the negatives; will they be offset by the positives? If there is some significant part of the duties that you will be expected to perform that is truly an anathema to you, you are probably better off to decline the offer. That is, unless you are in a truly desperate situation where you absolutely must have employment now.

Money is going to loom very large in your mind as you come out of school. There is an apartment to lease; perhaps a new car to buy. A vacation would surely be nice. A new wardrobe for the world of work is essential. Even so, money should not be the major determining factor.

Heed the commencement day advice from Bannus B. Hudson, chief executive officer of U. S. Shoe Corp., who told a 1994 graduating class: "The first thing you should try to do is find something (a job) you like. That's more important maybe than I thought when I got out of school. The temptation may be to find the best paying job or the first one that comes along. I think that's a terrible mistake."

It is a good idea, too, to ponder the advice of William Edward Burghardt Du Bois, noted Black American sociologist and author, who declared: "The return from your work must be the satisfaction which that work brings you and the world's need of that work. With this, life is heaven, or as near heaven as you can get. Without this – with work which you despise, which bores you, and which the world does not need – this life is hell."

Your task is to pick the best opportunity on a comparative basis. You also are not making a decision just for the immediate future. The first position you take along your career path and how well you perform in this assignment will have a significant influence on your longer-term future.

Any decision as important as this one is, deserves to be considered on an organized basis. You should methodically rate offers against the criteria you established earlier in the exercise when you were describing what you expect from your employer.

Four principles should guide your thinking:

(1) The job would be satisfying.

(2) The job would provide a good launching pad.

(3) The job would provide opportunities for growth.

(4) The job would provide reasonable compensation.

The work sheet that follows will be helpful in organizing the process for comparing offers against your goals, as well as one opportunity against the other(s).

RATING THE OPPORTUNITIES

(You should fill out one of these forms for each job offer being seriously considered. One is lowest; 10 is highest.)

Name of candidate employer _____

Date offer received _____

Outline of offer _____

_____

_____

_____

Overall reaction to organization and to offer _____

_____

_____

_____

Rate candidate employer and position offered on a scale of one to 10 in terms of the your expectations spelled out in the section of this book titled "What To Expect From Your Employer."

1 2 3 4 5 6 7 8 9 10

Environment of opportunity where
hard work and achievement are encouraged
and recognized. _____

Sensible risks encouraged. _____

Tools and resources provided. _____

Continuing education available. _____

<u>1 2 3 4 5 6 7 8 9 10</u>

Published, up-to-date personnel policies. _____

Quality products and services. _____

History of profitable growth. _____

Good work environment. _____

Growth/advancement opportunities. _____

Good corporate citizen. _____

Demonstrated willingness to change with times. _____

Open two-way communications practiced
within organization. _____

People encountered were positive
and businesslike. _____

"Gut" reaction to organization. _____

Would be proud to be associated
with the organization. _____

Location of job. _____

Competitive/satisfactory
compensation package. _____

TYPICAL QUESTIONS

However, your decision may be complicated by one or more questions. Here are some of the typical situations and some suggestions on how to deal with them.

What if I need more time to consider several offers?

Contact each person who has made an offer. Express your appreciation and enthusiasm. Be candid. Explain that you are very interested in this employer's offer, but that since it is such a big decision you need a little more time to consider your options. Set an absolute deadline for your decision.

If you favor this employer's offer, but still need a little more time to be 100 percent sure, don't hesitate to state your preference.

Recognize there is some risk involved in delaying the acceptance of an offer. A bird in the hand is worth two in the bush, according to the timeworn adage.

However, most employers will understand your position. If they don't and try to pressure you for an immediate decision or get impatient or even angry, you will learn a lot about the environment in which you might be working. Caution is the word.

What if I have an acceptable offer in hand, but there is another offer pending that I think would be even better if and when it comes through?

Consider the risk. Obviously, you can't tell those who have made the offers about this situation. You can ask for time as explained above. But don't let the courtship go on so long that it turns sour. You are the only one who can make the call on this one.

Can I negotiate a better deal?

Most employers have a rather firm fix on what they can offer for entry-level jobs. They also probably have more than one candidate on the line. As a result, in reality, you have very little room for negotiating the terms of your acceptance.

It is dangerous and foolish to run a bluff. However, this doesn't mean you should not make intelligent use of your strengths. Consider this situation: You, in fact, have offers from A and B that are basically comparable for compensation. A is offering more money, but overall you prefer to work for B. You should go back to B and explain the situation in detail.

"Frankly, Mr. B, all things considered, I would prefer to come to work for you, but I can't ignore the fact that A has offered me $5,000 more per year. I am not trying to pressure you, but as you can understand, I have to consider this difference. Are you in a position to increase your offer?"

While B may not match A's offer dollar for dollar, you may pick up some increase and there could be room to negotiate side issues. These would include time of reporting. (Don't say you want some time off.) Or moving expenses. If the company has numerous locations where your job would fit, you might discuss your place of employment.

What if I need more information?

Ask for it. If you feel another meeting with the key contact is in order, don't hesitate to request one. If you wish to meet with someone other than the primary interviewer, you may do so, but make this request with a keen sense of the pecking order.

ACCEPTING THE OFFER

When you have made up your mind, call your principal contact and accept the offer with great enthusiasm and without reservations. Show the same respect and attitude you exhibited during the interviewing process. Say you are ready to start work.

Explain that you will write a letter confirming your acceptance. Ask for a confirmation letter, with details of the offer, from the employer.

CLOSING THE FILE

Do not close your job search file until you have accepted a firm offer of employment in writing. It is a frightening thought, as suggested earlier, but what appears to be firm verbal offers do get denied. Situations change with employers and they have to back off on offers. So get it in writing.

Do not look back once you have accepted an offer. It is a mistake to second guess your decision. Do not compare your choice with ones made by your classmates or the person down the street. If you followed the suggested guidelines, you made a reasoned choice in selecting a job that will satisfy you for the time being.

Write a letter to everyone who made offers. Express your appreciation for their interest and their patience. Unless you are under some constraints from your soon-to-be employer, explain where you are going to work and what you will be doing.

Write similar letters to everyone on your job search team. Make a solemn oath to yourself that you will keep these people posted on your progress once you are on the job.

After you have written these letters, put your job search files in order and pack them away in a safe place.

These files and letters to those who helped you and those who offered employment opportunities are extremely important. In this volatile world you never know when you may need them again.

Congratulations and good luck!

You have successfully made your way over one of the toughest hills you will have to climb in your lifetime of work. You are off and running. It's up to you to make a success of this first full-time job.

(Examples of these "closing" letters are at the end of this book.)

PART TWO

YOUR UNOFFICIAL MANUAL FOR SUCCESS ON THE JOB

PART TWO *(Continued)*

YOU CAN MASTER THE JOB

Congratulations! You have landed that first full-time job. Your career has been launched. The outcome is up to you, no one else. You can swim with the winners and make a success of this job so that it is indeed the beginning of a rewarding and satisfying career. Or you can sink into that gray mass of also-rans or become an outright failure.

The remainder of this book is devoted to some basic rules of the career road. If you follow them they will make a difference in your work life. You will find that the underlying theme in all of them is hard work and common sense.

Sorry, there are no shortcuts. There is no pabulum here. This is in spite of the success gurus who would seduce us all with their siren calls. They counsel: "Visualize your goals, think positively, intimidate, manipulate, play the angles, lay back and let it happen. Voila, the deal is done. Success is inevitable. A Mercedes in the driveway, a condo in Aspen. Nothing is impossible."

It's easy to overdose on a plethora of books, tapes and seminars that promise to reveal in 12 easy lessons the keys to career success without risk or much effort and at a bargain price.

That's not the way it works. Loyalty, hard work and honesty of intent and action are still the keys that unlock the gate to a rewarding career.

The major reason people fail in their careers or fall short of their potential is their inability to deal with the real-world demands placed on all of us by the forces of organizational dynamics.

Organizational dynamics. Now that is a high flying phrase. Let's examine it in down-to-earth terms so it will do you some good. We are talking about how things get done…how people survive and prosper in organizations…how people relate one to another…how people are motivated and led. We are considering the forces – physical, fiscal, moral, human nature – that must be understood in any organization before any of us can accomplish much of anything and be successful in work life.

The organization you go to work for may give you a sort of *Official Manual* your first day on the job. Or there will be an orientation meeting. The purpose will be to spell out the rules and regulations that you are suppose to live by. There will be an imposing and probably confusing organization chart that shows who is boss and who reports to whom. All of that is important and necessary, of course.

However, you will soon recognize that the real organization operates outside the official book. Unfortunately, you won't be provided with a manual titled, "Unofficial Manual: This is the way it really works."

But you will have read HOW TO LAND YOUR FIRST JOB & MAKE A SUCCESS OF IT. It can be your Unofficial Manual. It will provide you with insights and advice about how to navigate your way through the world of organizations to achieve success in a competitive environment where knowing how to get things done is rewarded.

GET OFF ON THE RIGHT FOOT

Your career path begins on the first day you report for work. The importance of getting off on the right foot cannot be overstated.

Your boss is watching and measuring you, as are your colleagues. Face it, if your boss is halfway smart he wants you to succeed for his own sake. A few of your associates want you to succeed; some would like to see you fall on your face; the vast majority don't care. How well you do during the early days in establishing your person-to-person relationships within the organization, the attitudes you display toward work, and the skills you apply to your assignments, will provide strong and lasting indicators as to how you will progress.

Fair or unfair, those first impressions will have a lasting effect on how you will be rated. Who among us doesn't recall that professors were more likely to give us good grades all school year long if we made A pluses in September.

Work, work, work and then work some more. No substitute, no shortcut will replace work. This means more than working diligently from eight to five. Take work home, at least background reading, for nights and weekends. Immerse yourself in your work. Never miss a deadline and deliver what the boss orders, even though you may not agree with it.

Arrive early on the job and stay late. Get to work 30 minutes before the specified start-up time. Use this valuable period, before the interruptions begin, to get routine chores out of the way and lay out your tasks for the day.

Often, you will find your boss is in early. (That may have something to do with his being boss.) It's a great time to get better acquainted. Don't push it so far that you become a bug, but this is a good time to ask for extra information and guidance. With this leg up you will be able to do a better job and you will be seen by your boss as interested in your work.

Stay at least 15 minutes after the regular hours. Clean up your workplace. Pull out the files and reading material you want to take home for review each night. Make a "to do" list for the next day.

(You will learn more about being prepared in the following chapter: *Sunday Night Is The Most Important Night Of The Week.*)

Even though you realize the scoreboard is operating from day one don't expect to conquer the world in six months. Hit the ground running at a steady, sure pace, always moving toward your goal, at a speed you and the track you are on can handle. Odds are this strategy will keep you ahead of the pack.

Master the fundamentals, know the requirements and the limits of your job. Seek out responsibility, don't just sit back and wait for it. But never take on more than you can deliver in a first-class way.

Don't be afraid to ask questions and seek help when you have gone as far as you can on a project. Asking for help is a sign of strength, not of weakness as is often assumed. Seeking assistance, intelligently, shows you are confident and focused on getting the job done. Acquire a mentor as soon as possible. Find someone who has been over the course to provide coaching, share experiences and educate you on the culture of your workplace. It will not be hard to find at least one mentor to fill this role. Most people like to be asked for advice.

Observe how things really get done. Figure out what goes on in the blank spaces between the boxes and lines on the official organization chart. Learn who switches the gears and oils the machinery of the organization. You will soon recognize the truth that there is a big difference between what you read in the policy manual and what actually goes on.

Respect the hierarchy. The organization is bigger and stronger than you are; you can't change it in the beginning and maybe you never will be able to overhaul it. The sooner you accept this fact, the better. You have a boss and the chain of command is very real. You are not likely to make it as a rebel working outside the system.

Learn the business of the business, not just your job. Your first objectives, of course, are to learn your job and make the execution of it as good as possible. As soon as you have accomplished these goals, begin to educate yourself about the mission of the organization: what it does, what it sells and what values it represents; where it is positioned in its industry. Learn how your job fits into the scheme of things.

With this knowledge you will be able to perform more efficiently and you will enjoy your work more.

Adapt to the environment. Observe the style of dress – casual or more buttoned down? Adhere to it even if there is no official dress code.

Learn how business is done. Are decisions made and orders given by walking around and gathering in the coffee shop? Or are formal memoranda and meetings in conference rooms the favored methods?

According to the opinion polls, loyalty between employer and employee is on the wane. You will be smart to go counter to that trend. Be loyal to the organization that hands you a paycheck and in which you are launching your career. Loyalty to organizations may be disappearing, but this doesn't mean it is not still highly valued. When you progress to the point you have people reporting to you, what value will you place on loyalty? Being loyal to your employer will make you feel better about yourself and it will enable you to function more efficiently. Bottom line, loyalty will provide you with a competitive advantage.

Don't ever join cliques. They are *not good* for the health of your career. Especially, avoid choosing sides early in the game since you don't know where the skeletons are buried and you can't separate the winners from the losers.

Leave the gossip to others.

Recognize that politics do exist in the workplace. You can't avoid that fact. Approach the subject with extreme caution. You will read more about office politics in another chapter.

Nowhere is it written that you can't make progress in the world of organizations if you don't follow all of these rules. However, common sense and a lot of experience have clearly demonstrated to me that if you go contrary to them you raise the odds against your success and you make life more difficult. Do you need that?

SUNDAY NIGHT IS THE MOST IMPORTANT NIGHT OF THE WEEK

The reporter asked a routine question to begin his interview with the internationally-acclaimed marketing executive. He was startled by the answer he got.

"To what do you attribute your highly successful career'?" he asked.

"Sunday nights," came the surprising answer.

"Sunday nights? I don't understand what you mean," the reporter responded.

"It's just common sense, when you stop to think about it," the executive explained.

"I work hard every week from early Monday morning until late Friday afternoon. From Friday night until about mid-afternoon Sunday I take care of personal things and I play as hard as I work. I recharge my mind and body.

"Then I wind down the playing and devote Sunday night to preparing for the workweek ahead. I eat an early, sensible dinner. I review the previous week – my wins as well as my losses. Next, I go through my briefcase, reading everything that bears on the coming five days. I concentrate on what I want to accomplish during the week. I create my game plan. I set specific goals. I write a checklist with priorities clearly set out. While I'm at it, I also prepare one for my secretary."

He went on to explain how he even planned and prepared his wardrobe for the entire week, including putting a high shine on the shoes he would wear.

"All of this may sound a little strange," he said. "But I don't want anything to distract me from the important objectives I need to accomplish during the week at work."

He related how his preparation encompassed reading the Sunday newspapers and at least getting the gist of the information in the weekly news magazines.

"I know something will come up about current events during the week that will impact my job and I don't want to be caught short.

"Finally, I go to bed early, visualizing what I will accomplish during the week. I get a good night's sleep.

"When I walk into the office on Monday morning, I am already ahead of the game."

In a nutshell, this high achiever was talking about simple planning and preparation to make the best use of his time and energy.

This common sense idea seems about as obvious as the nose on your face. And it is, but not everyone recognizes the value of this sort of planning. Put it to work for yourself and you will beat the competition every time.

WINNING DEMANDS HARD WORK

It is always tempting to look at the winners in life and jump to the conclusion that they have been lucky enough to land feet first in a bed of roses.

But when you look behind the scenes of these seemingly charmed careers you are likely to find a different story, one of hard work, perseverance, and often pain.

Roger Staubach, the legendary quarterback of the Dallas Cowboys, is a good example of this truth.

Staubach won the Heisman Trophy, made All-American, and was named to the Pro-Football Hall of Fame. He was for many years the winningest quarterback in NFL history.

During an interview in his chief executive office at The Staubach Company in Dallas, I asked the superstar if it wouldn't be easy for his fans to think, "Roger's rich and famous. His life has been a piece of cake."

"I know a lot of people – particularly the younger ones – have that view, but it is a mistake," he replied. "Nothing has been handed to me. I am like everyone else. If you want to achieve your ambitions you have to pay a price."

Staubach points out that he faced many players in collegiate and professional competition who were bigger, faster and stronger. Several quarterbacks were blessed with quicker throwing arms.

Now a successful business executive and civic leader, he acknowledges the same kind of advantages in those he squares off against in the fiercely competitive world of real estate.

What then accounts for his record as a winner in life?

"Nobody works harder than I do," Staubach declares, simply and directly.

"I have always felt that work…combining your work with your talent gains results," he continues. "That's true in athletics and in business – in all walks of life. There are no short trips to success. I have seen a lot of talented people who haven't accomplished much."

When pressed to look at his own record of accomplishments, Staubach will say, "As an athlete, I gave everything I could mentally and physically. By doing so at various levels of my career I was passing by people who might have been smarter than I was or more talented. The difference was I was utilizing what I had to the fullest of my capabilities."

KEEP ON KEEPING ON

Achievers know that it takes more than ability, more than personality, even more than luck to win over the long haul.

These men and women realize they must have the persistence to "Keep On Keeping On," even when encountering setbacks and disappointments.

"Nothing in the world can take the place of perseverance," President Calvin Coolidge declared. "Talent will not; nothing is more common than unsuccessful men with talent. Genius will not; unrewarded genius is almost a proverb. Education will not; the world is full of educated derelicts. Persistence and determination alone are omnipotent."

One of life's big winners, Ted Turner, world-class sailor and founder of the CNN television network, explains his success by saying:

"The secret of my success is that I never quit. Winners never quit, and quitters never win. You might go bankrupt, you might lose everything, but as long as you're out there still duking back, as long as you haven't given up, you're not beaten. Many battles have been won in the eleventh hour. It might have looked like it was over. But the old saying is true: 'It's never over till it's over'."

People of all ages and walks of life who have made successes of their lives give a large share of the credit to their determination and persistence.

Allie Freeman, a former guard on the University of Arkansas basketball team and a winner in other endeavors on and off the campus, shares his success insights when he declares: "Determination means that you never give up. Dedication means you're going to take it, work with it, and work with it until you are really good at it."

Marathon runners provide some classic examples of persistence in achieving victory.

"Your body carries you the first 20 miles," explains Jim Johnson, vice chairman at Cranford Johnson Robinson Woods advertising, marketing and public relations agency. "Then you hit a point known by runners as 'the wall.' Your body has depleted its supply of fuel and you want to quit right there. But if you are going to go the full distance – the 26 miles – your brain has to take over from your body. You run on willpower. You get your mind right. You begin to set your goals in smaller bites. Where you started out thinking about your first goal of making it for 20 miles, now you are thinking about going another half mile, then a 100 yards and finally a few more steps. You have to gut it out."

Persistence is particularly important when things are going against you. And, of course, that is when it is hardest to remain focused on your goals and determined to reach them.

Polybius, a Greek historian, wrote, "Some men give up their designs when they have almost reached the goal; while others, on the contrary, obtain a victory by exerting, at the last moment, more vigorous efforts than before."

But common sense teaches that it is very important to understand the difference between *persistence* and *pigheadedness.*

Persistence is tenacity, the will and ability to "stick with it" until the goal is attained.

Pigheadedness means stubborn, obstinate, mulish. These are the ingredients for defeat.

Persistence is an act of both logic and faith. It means making sure the goal is worth the cost and believing that it is possible to reach it by making the best effort plus a little more.

Pigheadedness is to ignore reality and to beat one's head against a brick wall when the reward, even if it is won, is not worth the risk and effort.

Persistence, if it is to be constructive, has another side to it. That is having enough common sense to know when to drop a cause, when all of the facts say it is lost beyond hope, and move on to another goal. This positive force is all about winning wars, not just battles.

The critical difference is also knowing when your persistence has paid off the highest probable dividend. It is knowing when to be satisfied with a victory.

Good poker players know when to "hold 'em and when to fold 'em."

FORMULA FOR SUCCESS IS SIMPLE

The formula for success is really quite simple when you stop to think about it.

In fact, success requires only that you think of yourself as a merchant and your employer as your primary customer. Then, in this mindset, complete four basic steps, which anyone can take, given a reasonable amount of energy and intelligence.

They are:

(1) Provide a product or service that your customer wants to buy.

(2) Assure consistent quality.

(3) Guarantee a benefit to the buyer and full value for price paid.

(4) Make each transaction a pleasant and profitable experience, one to be repeated.

This formula applies whether or not you are making your career in a profession, working as a salaried employee in a corporation, serving as a salesperson in a retail shop, or trying to make it as the proprietor of a small business.

At this point, a common sense question begs to be answered. If it is so simple, why aren't more people successful?

Well, success does require commitment and hard work, extra effort and a burning desire to win. Success demands an orientation *outward* to the needs and desires of the market, rather than *inward* to your own immediate gratification.

The way to success is simple, but it is not easy. Not everyone is willing to pay the price.

Consider the ingredients for success, step by step.

How about providing the product or service your customer wants to buy?

A lot of us fail to provide this elementary requirement because we refuse to actually listen to the customer. We LISTEN, but we don't HEAR.

Many times, it is more convenient to provide the product we

already have on hand or the one we can turn out easily rather than go to the trouble to deliver what the customer wants. We are so busy serving our own needs and interests that we don't have any time or energy left over for the customer, who is the key to our success.

What's the story on quality and "value for price paid"?

Quality is strictly discretionary – always. It gets left out sometimes when we try to gain a quick profit by cutting a corner on the ingredients we put in the product. Quality goes missing when we don't have the interest or the energy to stay an extra half hour after the shop closes to check the shipping list or to proofread the memorandum going to the boss.

Perhaps the easiest of all the elements in the success formula is the one having to do with attitude: "smile…be friendly." Anyone can make it "a pleasure to do business."

Take the most obvious example of this reality. Salespersons in retail stores usually work on commission. Their success is a direct line from what they sell to what they earn.

It doesn't take a brain surgeon to figure out that the friendlier and more helpful a salesperson is the more they will sell and the more they will earn (i.e. the more successful they will be).

Being courteous takes very little effort. It is the difference between "What do you want?" and "How may I help you?" It's the difference between ignoring the waiting customer while finishing the joke with another member of the staff or moving briskly to help the would-be buyer find the correct size dress in the desired color.

When all is said and done, our personal success depends directly on our being driven by a goal of delivering benefits for those to whom we sell our products and services rather than serving our immediate interest.

Anyone of us can be successful. It is a matter of individual, personal choice. Take success or leave it.

THERE IS NO SUCH THING AS A ROSE GARDEN WITHOUT THORNS

You may think you have landed squarely in the middle of a blooming rose garden when you get your first job. But remember there is no such thing as roses without thorns.

You just hit a home run; you landed the job you wanted. Enjoy the euphoria for a few days. Expect it to wear a bit thin. Sooner or later you will hit a slump in your feelings and begin to have second thoughts: Why did I come here? Have I made a mistake? Don't feel badly. That is par for the course.

Be prepared for some surprises. You will find that the organization doesn't look the same from the inside as it did from the outside when you and your employer were engaged in the mating dance. When you are disappointed and even discouraged, remind yourself that if the organization had been perfect there would have been no need to hire you.

Be realistic about the reception you receive. There will be many signs of cordiality, most of them sincere. Accept them graciously, but remember that even in the best of circumstances honeymoons don't last forever. Be aware that beneath the surface there is another world with tensions and competition.

You will be on trial for some time to come as the organization takes your measure. Your associates, even your boss, will still be dealing with the same question: what does his or her coming here mean to me?

Hasten to establish your competence. Strange as it may seem, you need to reassure your boss that you are on the job to help him. Show your peers that while you are a team player, you understand your responsibilities and the extent of your authority. Let them know you intend to fulfill each.

You will have an objective view of the situation in the early days that you will never have again. The personalities, the pressures, the gains and losses you will certainly encounter will color your thinking as time goes by. Take time now to spell out in writing how you see the situation, the tasks you have been assigned, the pluses as well as the minuses. Describe how you feel about the people you work with, especially your boss. State your goals, immediate and long term.

Refer to this document frequently. Prepare updated versions from time to time, but always use your initial impressions as the benchmark. This process will help you maintain your objectivity about yourself, the organization and those with whom you work.

BE SURE IT IS TRUE AMBITION GNAWING AT YOUR INSIDES

It is easy to be confused and distracted by ambition. So be sure you know the true meaning of ambition and how to handle it.

Ambition is a sanctified ideal in the folklore of career success. Just the word – as in "She has always been ambitious" – evokes a degree of respect and admiration.

However, in practice, ambition is like most icons. It is not a good and positive force in and of itself. Ambition may be embraced or ignored; used or abused. It can even become an excuse for failure. All of this depends on how it is employed.

The true meaning of ambition goes beyond the dictionary definition.

"Ambition is not dreaming and talking about where I want to go, when I want to get there. Ambition is knowing where I want to go and how to get there, plus being willing to do what it takes to reach the goal," says Craig Douglas, a communications consultant in Little Rock, Arkansas.

"The key is to combine ambition, which means desire, with initiative, which means action," he concludes.

Some valuable lessons can be learned from the story of Bruce Tucker.

A very bright and intelligent young man, Bruce had been in his job less than one year. He was already restless and frustrated by what he saw as a lack of progress.

"I am ambitious. I will be a success, but I will never make it doing these little insignificant things day in and day out. I could do a lot more; my boss just won't give me a chance," he declared.

Bruce had demonstrated he was well educated to make a good career in sales. Shirley Carpenter, his supervisor, believed the young man had potential, which hopefully could be developed and saved for the company. But his constant complaining was getting to be a problem.

Shirley called Bruce in for a performance evaluation and discussion. The meeting soon turned into a sour confrontation when Bruce once again began to push his ambitions.

"I am still doing the same old things. I know I am paid less than the others in the department. It's just not fair," he said, ignoring the compliments he had been paid at the start of the conference.

"Bruce, you have been with us for only eleven months," Shirley explained patiently. "You are the newest salesperson; everyone else has been here at least three years. They have worked their way up the ladder.

"You are making fine progress, but let's face it, you are still short on experience. Give it a little more time. If you hang in there, you will make it."

Shirley complimented Bruce again and went on to suggest that his work habits needed some improvements.

"Bruce, you are late most mornings, and you are out of here right at five o'clock every day," Shirley said. "And, frankly, I think you could improve your performance by devoting a little time at night and on the weekend to learning more about your job."

"You are not being fair," Bruce bristled. "The company is not paying me as much as it pays the rest of you. I work the hours you pay me for. Sure, I see you and the others staying late, but I don't have anything to do, and, besides, as I told you, I am not married to this company. You pay me and I will show you what I can do."

Bruce then spelled out what he expected the company to do to meet his ambitious expectations.

"I am ambitious," he reiterated. "I expect to be a group manager in six months. I just can't wait around forever."

Shirley saw the discussion was dead-ending, but she still believed Bruce had potential and could be saved. Shirley made what she thought was a fair offer.

"Let's expand your responsibilities," she offered. "You become an assistant group manager. Work with Jim Davis. He is the best we have and you can learn a lot from his experience. We will provide you with some special training. However, I can't give you a raise right now since our budgets are frozen, but I will when I can if you continue to do a good job. In fact, I can promise you a raise in four to six months."

"Again, Shirley, you are not being fair to me," Bruce charged. "Everyone in the department knows Jim Davis is past his prime. He is worn out. I would be running his errands. What could I learn from him? I would just be the laughingstock of the office. I don't think that is much of a promotion. It certainly is not what I deserve."

Bruce never recovered from that discussion in the eyes of his supervisor and the department head who had been briefed on the tragedy as it unfolded.

Bruce failed to learn anything from the episode about the real meaning of ambition. Instead, he used his ambition as an excuse for failure, telling everyone things hadn't worked out at the company because he was "too ambitious to wait around in that archaic outfit to be promoted."

MANAGE YOUR BOSS TO MANAGE YOUR CAREER

Your career will kick into overdrive the day you begin to act on the inescapable truths about bosses.

Everybody has a boss. You are no exception. You will have a boss on your first job. You will have a boss if you get to be the chief executive officer, commanding the corporate jet and cashing the stock options.

In order to reach your potential you must learn how to manage your boss.

A boss is a human being, although that may be hard to realize some days.

On any given day, a boss can appear as a parent who is respected, feared, or barely tolerated. A boss can be seen as a competitor, a block in the way of progress. He or she can be a hero or a bum. A boss can be accepted as a wise and kindly teacher or a critical taskmaster. A boss may not always be right, but the boss is always boss.

The next five chapters deal with nurturing and managing the all-important relationship between you and your boss.

EVERYBODY HAS A BOSS

The ink was hardly dry on Tom Meredith's MBA degree before he landed a desirable job with a "hot" new firm. The sixth and last person to join the staff, he was in on the ground floor. His future looked promising.

Six weeks later, he had either quit or been "let go."

Here's his version of what went wrong.

He did not like his boss, who, he said, had been unfair and un-willing to give him all of the responsibility he could handle. The place was poorly managed, he thought.

"My boss and the others in the office didn't respect me," Tom declared. "I was always the one who had to get coffee for meetings. I wasn't getting to meet the clients except when I was bringing in the coffee and donuts. It was demeaning."

Now middle-aged, the man has yet to find success or satisfaction in his work. Chances are he never will.

The truth behind this tragedy of wasted talent is that he failed to accept a simple irrefutable fact of life. Wherever we go there is always a hierarchy. We will always have a boss – someone in authority who directs our activities, whose approval we must secure to survive and succeed. Organizations can't exist without a chain of command.

Managers report to directors. Vice presidents report to executive vice presidents. Presidents report to chairmen of the board. Entrepreneurs are responsible to those who finance their businesses. Doctors are accountable to patients, as lawyers are to clients. "Mom and Pop" running the neighborhood quick stop, have some of the toughest bosses in the world, their customers.

A Danish zoologist proved that even in the barnyard chickens work within the reality of a strong hierarchy. There is always a top chicken in the yard. Mr. Big can peck anybody. The second level chicken can peck the third level, and so it goes. It's called the "pecking order."

Living with the "pecking order" is often difficult for most of us. After all, the very origin of the term "boss" is the Dutch word "bass" which means "master." Few achievers like the notion of having a master. Accepting authority is basically at odds with many of the attributes of success, such as self-confidence, the desire to reach out aggressively for responsibility, and the ability to move steadily toward a goal.

The achieving of a successful career does not require that you like the idea of having a boss. You don't even have to like your boss, although it helps. But common sense says you have to accept the idea of a boss and learn to deal positively with this fact of life if you are going to achieve success.

A study of successful careers suggests some strategies that help.

1. You should make every effort to respect your boss, his experience and his position. Hopefully, you will be respected in return.

2. Don't rely on an "office friendship" with your boss. Diogenes, the Greek philosopher, had some good advice about this point: " A man should live with his superiors as he does with his fire; not too near, lest he burn; not too far, lest he freeze."

3. Never, never go around or over your boss. Work with and through him.

   You may believe him to be incompetent and a roadblock to all the great things you could accomplish. That may be correct, but you put yourself in extreme danger if you elect to try the end run.

   You can bet the hierarchy will close ranks to protect itself from such violations of protocol.

(The only exception is when you *know for certain* that the superior is involved in some deliberate action that is causing material damage to the organization. Even then, when you act, you must be prepared to "seek other opportunities.")

Organizations do not take kindly to those who break rank, for whatever reasons.

4. Always try to make your boss look good in the eyes of his boss and the system as a whole. Work diligently to get him promoted. If you succeed, room will be created for you to move up in your department. Or you will be identified by the organization as a real hitter, and be put on the "A-List" for promotion elsewhere in the organization. Or maybe you will be spotted by another employer. In any case, you can start all over to make a hero of your new boss.

Remember, you don't have to like your boss. But you do need to respect the position he holds and honor your responsibility to your employer. The better your boss makes out the better you will make out.

BOSSES MAKE MISTAKES, TOO

The boss is always the boss, but that doesn't mean he or she is always right.

You are well served in your career when you accept this truth and learn to deal constructively with it. Your boss and the organization that employs both of you will also be better off.

Bosses often have a way of appearing infallible. In fact, it is easier for them to be right, or appear to be right, than it is for those whom they supervise. Bosses have access to more data and resources. They have more control over circumstances. Moreover, we tend to assume (often with a little nudging from them) that they are always right. Still, bosses do make mistakes.

A primary responsibility of subordinates is to help their bosses to avoid making mistakes and to correct errors once they are committed.

If you are working for a boss who will not entertain the idea he could be wrong some of the time and refuses to accept suggestions for corrective actions, you are in a losing situation.

This lesson was taught again when the international securities firm of Shearson Lehman suffered what was then the largest quarterly loss in the history of Wall Street ($630 million).

Those close to the disaster said it came about largely because no one in the organization was strong enough to tell Peter Cohen, the chairman, that he was wrong.

One insider said that Cohen's senior associates failed to speak up because they were too busy trying to figure out "what Peter wants."

Some bosses want to blame others. They are like the humorist James Thurber, who made a mistake in placing a telephone call and then demanded of the person who answered and told him he had the wrong number, "Well, if I called the wrong number, why did you answer the phone?"

It is not easy to tell the boss he is wrong. Even under the best of circumstances, most bosses don't relish hearing that message. But then who does? Nevertheless, bosses (and subordinates) who are going to be successful will grit their teeth, hear the truth, and take corrective actions.

Of course, so much depends on how the message is delivered. Obviously, it is not wise to simply declare, "Boss, you are wrong."

Sometimes, it is best to correct a supervisor's mistake by not carrying out an order or by procrastinating until the situation cools down. This is particularly effective if your boss is given to temper fits during which he acts rashly. It is, however, a risky course of action.

In a rage, President Kennedy ordered the chairman of the Federal Communications Commission to punish the NBC television network, through whatever means possible, for a news report it had broadcast. The FCC head sat on the order and did nothing for several days. He then told Mr. Kennedy what he had (not) done, making the point that The President was fortunate to have people working for him who were too loyal to carry out every order posthaste. By that time, JFK had cooled down and agreed with the tactic.

Before telling the boss he is wrong be sure the mistake is worth the effort to correct it. Some mistakes just don't make any difference unless, of course, they give you an *unbearable* pain in the backside. If the problem is material, bite the bullet and speak up.

When you have to report an error, make the message as impersonal as possible. Do not become accusatory. Be sure you have the facts to support your case and stick to them.

Wrap the message in diplomatic language. "Have you noticed that…?" "What would happen if we took another approach?" "I am not being critical, but…" "I know you would want me to tell you about…"

Always have a suggestion for corrective action or a better way to do something so the mistake won't be repeated.

Offer to help.

Take your fair share, and more, of the responsibility if you have had a role in creating the error.

Finally, remember, this is not a game of "gotcha" in which you see how many times you can catch the boss in a mistake. Don't keep score.

NEVER LET YOUR BOSS BE SURPRISED

There is only one thing worse than delivering bad news to your boss. That is not delivering bad news when you know trouble is brewing.

It is a cardinal sin to let your boss be caught by surprise. (The same commandment applies in your dealings with customers, those whom you supervise, and your peers.)

Cleaning up a vulgar bit of bumper-strip philosophy, "Bad news happens." No one and no organization escapes it forever. Budgets are not met. Deliveries are late. Machines don't work. People are caught with their hands in the cookie jar.

It is important to your career success to learn how to deliver bad news, as well as how to receive it.

(You will learn more about what to do when you make a mistake in a later chapter.)

There are at least five major things wrong with failing to blow the whistle when you see bad news coming.

First, ignoring bad news won't make it go away. It's bound to surface sooner or later, probably at the worst possible time.

Second, most problems can be fixed, wholly or in part, if addressed soon enough. You deny your boss and the organization that opportunity when you try to hide the bad tidings.

Third, left unattended, most problems simply get bigger and more difficult with time.

Fourth, when you fail to report the bad news you are leaving your boss vulnerable to being blindsided with a problem and the accusation from his boss that he doesn't have control of his organization.

Fifth, you are even more vulnerable to these hazards than the boss is.

Paul Gordon was placed in charge of the small publishing division of a large corporation. It was his breakthrough opportunity.

Things appeared to be going along according to plan for several months. Sales to wholesalers for the two major magazines were strong and encouraging.

133

But then bad news began to appear on the horizon. Wholesalers were reporting that the magazines weren't selling off the news-stands. They began returning the unsold stock, which they had taken on consignment.

Fearful of what the reversals might mean to the undertaking, to say nothing of his reputation, Paul put off going to his immediate supervisor, Betty Johnson. Finally, when he reported the bad news to Betty, the two of them decided to sit on the ominous signs, believing that things would get better. They didn't. The trickle of returns became an avalanche. Dollar losses were alarming.

Now Paul and Betty were in real trouble. Paul knew he should have reported the problem to Betty much sooner. Betty in turn recognized she had failed to alert her boss in a timely manner. As luck would have it, Paul and Betty were scheduled to appear before the executive committee to report on the outlook for the publishing venture as a prelude to an expansion proposal.

The day before the report was due, a corporate auditor revealed the grim numbers to the chief financial officers, who in turn went immediately to the company president.

In a rage of disappointment, the company president demanded that Paul and Betty be relieved of their responsibilities for the publishing venture. A red flag was put on both of their files in the human resources department. The publishing division was sold three months later.

Paul and Betty learned later that had they reported the problem in its early stages, the executive committee probably would have given them the time and resources needed to correct the problem.

Both left the company within a few months.

Don't expect to be a hero when you have to report bad news. Chances are you will take some bruises. In ancient times, kings cut off the heads of messengers who brought bad news.

You may not lose your head, but don't be surprised if the boss erupts into a Class A rage. But that is still better than the Class AA anger that is likely to rain down on you if you have tried to hide the bad news that will surely surface later.

There is really no good way to report the bad news; however, you can take some steps to help ease the pain.

Have all of the facts in hand. Report them succinctly; no fooling around.

Be patient; let the boss vent his or her anger and frustration.

Offer a solution, or at least some way to cut the losses.

If you are to blame, take the heat yourself; don't try to lay it off on others. If a group of which you are a part is at fault be sure you report in the "we" mode. Don't be defensive. If some other individual or group is clearly to blame, report the facts, but be gentle. Try to depersonalize the matter.

Be sure you have made a practice of reporting good news, too. Avoid being identified as one who always bears ill tidings.

Hopefully, you are working for an organization like Bank of America, no stranger to bad news, which is said to operate by the rule, "Kill the messenger only if he's late with the news."

FEW THINGS ARE MORE DIFFICULT THAN AN INSECURE BOSS

You will find few things more difficult to deal with during your career than a boss who is insecure. Unfortunately, it is a near certainty that you will encounter one or more such persons along the way.

But think of it this way. Do you really want a superior who is so self-assured (make that arrogant) that he thinks he is always right?

The symptoms of the debilitating malady are easy to spot. Unless treated effectively, insecurity will spread throughout the entire organization, creating an unhappy and ineffective environment.

You will know your boss is suffering from insecurity when he or she is engaging in behavior highlighted by such traits as the following:

The boss insists on absolute control over everything in the department. He rules with an iron hand, refusing to delegate any real authority. He doesn't trust anyone. He has few allies. Those allies he does enlist are formed into a tight little clique strongly obligated to his authority and dependent on it. They live an uncertain life on a short leash.

The boss constantly interferes in your work. Second guesses are the order of the day.

Another trait is that he will defend his position at even the hint of a challenge. Every question or hint of criticism is treated as a challenge to his worth and authority. He doubts he has the respect of those around him. Those associates who exhibit a mind of their own are under constant attack.

The insecure boss is most often an absolute perfectionist. He will climb the wall when you make a mistake. But look out. When he fouls up, he will blame it on someone else. He has to be right every time.

He will resist making decisions. This means endless studies and return trips to the drawing boards.

He will frequently remind you who's boss.

And when your superior suffers from insecurities he will find it next to impossible to laugh at himself, but he is ready to laugh at others.

The symptoms of an insecure boss will eventually create an insecure organization, riddled with anxiety and indecision. People will spend more time looking over their shoulders than looking ahead. Good defenses become more important than effective offenses.

What actions can you take if your boss fits this troublesome category? There are no certain quick fixes, but there are some steps to help mitigate the situation and advance your own interests. Actually, insecure bosses can offer opportunities.

First, be certain you are not contributing to your superior's low self-esteem. Be sure everything you do reassures him of your respect for his position and your commitment to helping him get his job done.

Shore him up at every opportunity. Learn where he feels most insecure – where the hot buttons are – and make a special effort to be helpful in these areas.

When you have to challenge him, and surely you will from time to time, be certain to do it in a positive way. Never challenge or criticize the boss in the presence of others.

Never go around your insecure boss to deal directly with his boss without explicit approval. Make sure he realizes that you clearly understand the hierarchical relationships. You don't want to become an endangered species because you are seen as appealing to higher authorities.

Always be sure he gets more than his fair share of credit for your good work. Stay one step behind him when the limelight shines.

Remember, your boss may be a pain in the neck to work with, but surely he must have some redeeming features worthy of compliments. Find some good points and lay them on him.

That is just common sense at work. Be sensitive. Think of your own insecurities and what helps you deal with them. Apply what you learn from this exercise to dealing with your insecure boss.

CONFLICTS WITH YOUR BOSS ARE NATURAL

If you are a proactive, get-things-done person who has what it takes to succeed, sooner or later you will come in conflict with your boss. This fact of career life is as certain as the sun rising in the East.

Looked at another way, if you do not have periodic disagreements with your supervisors, you are probably not being as assertive as you should be in moving your career ahead.

After all, it was the same kind of confidence and strong will that made your boss the boss that will propel you to rise in the organization. Strong forces are bound to collide.

Times of conflict are stressful for everyone involved. They can damage your working relationships and prove hazardous to the health of your career. But if these encounters are handled with common sense, they don't have to come to that sort of end.

Knowing you will have these differences if you are making progress in your career, you should be prepared to handle them so there are no individual losers.

Here are some suggestions for handling the inevitable run-ins with your boss.

1. Determine what is really at stake and how important it is to the parties involved, including your employer. If, upon calm reflection, it is not truly important beyond the possibility of your feelings being bruised, forget it. Save your energies for another time when the stakes are higher. Recall the Chinese proverb that holds it is not worth setting your house on fire to get rid of your mother-in-law, especially if she can eventually make you rich.

2. Define the issue in the conflict. Do it in writing so that you (and perhaps others later) have a concise understanding as to what the controversy is all about.

3. Give full consideration to the boss's point of view. Remember, his responsibilities are different than yours. He may have a

legitimate reason for his opinion, which you are not aware of at the moment. The conflict you see may disappear with an explanation or the passage of time.

4. Weigh your side of the argument against the good of the organization. Before you "go to the mat" on an issue, be sure you are motivated by what you believe to be the larger interests and not your own narrowly-defined agenda.

5. If after all of this thought, you still feel the difference is worth an open disagreement with your boss, carefully prepare your case. If it is truly a major issue, ask for a face-to-face discussion. If the matter is not resolved at that time, ask permission to leave a written explanation of your point of view with your boss.

   For differences of less magnitude, try to make your point of view known and reach a solution with an exchange of memoranda.

6. Never push your boss into a corner where he can only win or lose. There is almost always more than one correct answer to any problem. Try to find an acceptable resolution between conflicting points of view.

7. Avoid letting the matter be positioned on a personal basis. Emotions and personalities have no place in a confrontation with the boss.

8. Be tactful. Show respect for the boss's position and responsibilities. Whatever the outcome, he will still be your organizational superior when the smoke clears.

9. Keep it in perspective. It is good to remember that win, lose or draw, it is a rare situation when the resolution of an issue results in a pot of pure gold at the end of the rainbow or the world coming to an end.

10. Don't pin a medal on your chest if you prevail. By the same token, don't wear the black of mourning if the decision goes against you. Keep it to yourself either way and go on with your job.

11. If you have had your day in court and the boss still doesn't agree, be a good trooper, support his decision openly and aggressively.

12. Keep a personal account of the conflicts with your boss. If you can't openly discuss your differences with him and arrive at acceptable resolutions, or if these disagreements are so frequent and painful that your life and career are being disrupted, recognize you have a problem larger and more critical than any single issue. It may be you are at odds with the standards and objectives of your boss or even the organization as a whole.

Explore your options if you find yourself in this situation. Find a way to reduce the conflict in your present position, or locate another opportunity. Life is too short to live constantly in a world of turmoil and confrontation that are not ultimately rewarding.

HOW TO HANDLE RESPONSIBILITY

You have three options when it comes to handling responsibilities. The choice you make on your first job is one of the most powerful determinants of the kind of success you will achieve in your career.

One option is to *avoid responsibility* whenever possible. After all, responsibility does entail risk and more work. People in the military learn early "don't volunteer," that is unless they want to make a career of the armed services.

The outcome of this course of action is predictable. Avoiding responsibility is certain to mean staying in place, and eventually drifting downward into the routine of the bureaucracy.

A second option is to *accept responsibility* when it is thrust upon you. The commonly-accepted wisdom is that this is the road to success.

To sit back and just accept responsibility when you are sought out means remaining in the gray middle with a lot of people who will exist as good soldiers, but never as real leaders.

But smart careerists understand that *avoiding* responsibility is deadly or even just *accepting* responsibility is not enough. The key to getting ahead of the competition is to aggressively *seek* responsibility. This means to literally seize responsibility wherever it is left untended.

That is the way to move ahead of the competition. And it is not difficult to do because most people are happy to take one of the first two options.

However, a word of caution is in order here.

The aggressive, upwardly-mobile man or woman also knows that the reach for responsibility should never exceed the grasp – the ability to handle it.

Jim Robinson, former chief executive officer of American Express, admonished his colleagues to "Promise only what you can deliver and deliver what you promise."

If you have what it takes to be a winner in the career chase, you are possessed by an almost irresistible urge to take on more and more assignments. But assuming additional responsibilities until there is an impossible overload is a sure road to a big headache, if not worse.

The scenario is predictable.

If your supervisor has seen you perform as a reliable, ambitious producer, he will be only too glad to let you take on more and more. However, he may not recall all that is already on your plate.

So he gives you another assignment. You accept it and he expects you to do your usual good job on time. But if you are so overloaded that you don't get the work done on time and up to expectations, he forgets what you have done for him lately.

His chagrin and disappointment will not be lessened by the excuse, "I have had so much to do. I have been here every night until 10 or 11 o'clock."

Lou Gerstner, chief executive officer of IBM (after serving as CEO of RJR Nabisco and president of American Express), says ambitious people need to learn early on that it is perfectly acceptable to decline an assignment when they know they cannot deliver on time and up to standards because of an overload. That is, he says, if they are recognized producers.

Far better, declares Gerstner, to say up front, "Sorry, although I would like to do that job for you, I am so overloaded right now that I simply can't deliver the kind of quality you and I want on the schedule you need. Can you give me a little more time or can we delay delivery of another one of my assignments?"

The message is clear with regard to responsibilities. Reach out and grasp all you can handle. But once you take an assignment there is absolutely no viable excuse for not completing it as promised.

Your answers to three questions will reveal a great deal about how you handle responsibility and will provide a sure indicator of the direction and pace of your career.

1. When you have finished an assignment, do you wait for your leader to give you another one or do you go looking for your next task?

2. Do you carry your full load of assignments and offer to do more?

3. Are you looking ahead to the challenge of increasingly difficult responsibilities?

LEARN TO LOSE TO WIN

The idea of winning is at the very heart of the American ethic. In fact, this attitude toward competition has become almost a national mania. The gospel of our cultures, as handed down by professional football coach Vince Lombardi, the high priest of competition, held that winning is not just the best thing…it is the only thing.

The fact of the matter is that in real life, everyone – no matter how smart, ambitious, and deserving – is going to lose some of the time.

Consider the writings of Wilfred A. Peterson:

"The wise man realistically accepts failures as a part of life and builds a philosophy to meet them and make the most of them. He lives on the principle of 'nothing attempted, nothing gained' and is resolved that if he fails he is going to fail while trying to succeed."

If you want to be one of the ultimate winners in life you have to understand and be prepared to deal with this equation. You must get in the game in order to have a chance to win. If you are in the game, playing to win, you are taking risks. If you are taking risks you are certain to suffer some losses. The key is to get enough hits among the strikeouts to end up ahead when the game is over.

This is often a difficult proposition to accept, especially if you were one of the army of youngsters who shivered in your oversized Little League uniform while some hyperventilating adult screamed at you for committing such gross offenses as dropping pop flies and striking out.

Those who feel they have to win every time develop an inhibiting fear of risks. Do nothing, play it safe. So they hang back from participating because they are afraid they may lose. They are subject to a paralyzing neurosis, the symptoms of which are fear and self-doubt. The result is foreordained: they never even have a chance to win because they don't try.

Dr. Harry Levenson, noted psychologist and adviser to management, believes that a key characteristic of successful managers is the willingness to take substantial risks of losing.

"Not crazy risks, but big risks," he says. "They are willing to endure the distress of fear and uncertainty until the results are known. They stick with their decisions even when there are some downers before their ideas begin to pay off. They envision outcomes that others, without the same range of perception, cannot see. Then, they act on those visions of what is possible."

The achievers are willing to take risks because they know they do not have to win every battle to win the war. Fact is, it is not necessary to win every point. It is a very rare situation that has only one right answer. One instance would be disarming a live bomb. Another might be brain surgery. Otherwise, several acceptable options usually exist for each problem.

R. H. Macy failed seven times before his first store caught on. Babe Ruth struck out 1,330 times, but he is in the Hall of Fame because he also hit 714 home runs.

Anyway, you can't win all of the time, no matter how hard you try. You just need to be sure you win enough of the big ones.

Winners understand that failing to win does not necessarily mean losing. *There is a big difference between a loss and a defeat.*

Thomas Edison recorded some 25,000 failures in his attempt to invent a storage battery. "Those were not failures," he insisted. "I learned 25,000 ways not to make a battery."

When launching a project, winners plan to win, but they also have a standby strategy for what they will do to recover and gain new ground in case they lose.

MBA candidates at the University of Pennsylvania got the word from Raymond W. Smith, top gun at Bell Atlantic Corporation:

"Taking the safe road, doing your job, and not making waves may not get you fired (right away, at least), but it sure won't do much for your career or your company over the long haul. We (top managers) know that administrators are easy to find and cheap to keep. Leaders – risk takers – are in very short supply. And ones with vision are pure gold."

The real winners know something else about winning and losing. Even if you could win everytime, you shouldn't. In fact, strange as it seems, they know that learning how to lose is the key to learning how to win. They have mastered the art of losing strategically, in their career relationships.

If you insist on winning every single point, you set up opposition. Let's face it, nobody likes anyone who always wins.

Unless you are absolutely sure you have the only correct answer, or that your organization will be materially injured if you don't prevail, you should let your associates win a few. This is especially true if the others include your boss or your subordinates. The abilities of both will be improved, as will their morale.

But when common sense and facts say yours is clearly the best or only acceptable solution, you should fight for it with tooth and class.

Winning is not a zero sum matter. There does not have to be a loser for every winner. If you win, it is just common sense to make sure others feel they won, too.

If you truly want to build a successful career – and are willing to pay the price – but you work in an organization that demands that you always be right, you are probably in trouble. Such an environment will not allow you room to grow and achieve success. You will either be stifled or in trouble for trying new ideas and making the inevitable mistakes that go with them. You should get out when you can do so advantageously, unless you want to live in a suffocating bureaucracy.

You should be particularly wary of the organization that loudly calls for risk taking, while expecting a hit every time you come to bat. Perfect is not normal.

David Ogilvy, a superstar in the advertising business, tells the story of a toy buyer at Sears who made a mistake that cost his company $10 million. When Ogilvy asked the man's boss if he planned to fire the erring buyer, he replied, "Hell no. I fire people who never make mistakes because they never take chances and they never accomplish much."

A former chairman of Koppers Company told his associates, "Make sure you generate a reasonable number of mistakes."

These anecdotes simply say that wise persons know progress is not possible without risks; risks are not possible without mistakes. Healthy, growing organizations – the kind you want to be with – expect their people to make some mistakes. But not too many, mind you.

Be willing to take some common sense risks. Be ready to lose some of the time in order to be a big winner in the end.

SO YOU MADE A MISTAKE

Of course, mistakes are important. But the fact that you made a mistake is not nearly as important as what you do about it.

This is true, because the way you follow up on the errors will probably have a greater impact on the future of your career than what you did or didn't do wrong.

That's hard to believe when you are wallowing in the bed of regret, second-guessing and even fear that usually follows on the heels of a mistake.

It is worthwhile to restate the axiom that everyone makes mistakes. More precisely, everyone who is making an effort to get things done makes mistakes.

The Coca Cola Company, thought by many to be the smartest marketer in the world, made a major mistake when it decided the world needed a new flavor of its favorite beverage. Ford Motor Company pulled off a "Lulu" by producing a dud, the Edsel automobile. Kodak lost its complete dominance of the world of photography when it failed to anticipate Polaroid. And then Polaroid fell back due to a series of mistakes presided over by its founder, Edwin L. Land.

So mistakes are bound to occur, even among the best of us.

Smart careerists learn early in the race to capitalize on mistakes by turning them into learning experiences.

William Smithburg, chairman of Quaker Oats Company, told a group of food marketers, "There isn't one senior manager in this company who hasn't been associated with a product that failed, or some project that failed. That includes me. It's like learning to ski. If you're not falling down, you're not learning."

The writer William Saroyan declared, "Good people are good because they've come to wisdom through failure. We get very little wisdom from success, you know."

The next time you make a mistake keep in mind the following steps that achievers take when they "goof up."

If the situation permits the time, stop long enough to clear your head. Get the facts so you can define the mistake. Outline its parameters. What is the worst thing that can happen? The best? Will the mistake really make any difference one week, one year, five years later?

Don't panic. Follow the admonition of the television commercial for a deodorant, "Never Let Them See You Sweat."

Admit the failure. Report it to the boss. It is far better for you to tell him or her about your mistake than to have it come from others, who may or may not report it accurately. Help the boss keep it in perspective. Never attempt to cover up a mistake. Remember, it is a cardinal sin to allow your boss to be surprised.

A Confucian proverb advises, "Be not ashamed of mistakes and thus make them crimes."

Accept the responsibility for your mistakes. It is dishonest to try to lay off your mistakes on someone else. Besides that, such an action will come back to haunt you sooner or later.

(If an associate makes a mistake, keep in mind the humanizing bit of philosophy laid down by Alexander Pope, "To err is human, to forgive is divine.")

It's okay to feel the pain. Mourn a little if it is a big mistake. You will feel better later. Let the boss and your colleagues know you regret the error. Nothing is likely to infuriate your supervisor more than your appearing not to care when you make a mistake.

Act decisively, *pronto*. Don't just sit there shaking your head. Decide what has to be done and act to correct the problem before it mushrooms.

When things are back on track, do a postmortem. How did the mistake occur and why? How can a repeat performance be avoided? What did you learn from the experience? How can you do a better job?

You would be wise to take a page from the book of James Burke, who was CEO at Johnson & Johnson when seven people died after taking the company's Tylenol product which had been laced with cyanide. He advises friends faced with big-time bad news, "Be contrite and honest. And tell the public and regulators about the mistakes – no matter how bad – as quickly as you can."

Then forget the mistake, but remember the lesson learned.

The only truly unforgivable mistake is to repeat a mistake.

Mary Pickford, the actress, said, "If you have made mistakes, even serious mistakes, there is always another chance for you. And supposing you have tried and failed again and again, you may have a fresh start any moment you choose, for this thing that we call 'failure' is not the falling down, but the staying down."

TIME IS THE ENEMY OF US ALL

During a poignant scene in Tennessee William's play, "Sweet Bird of Youth," the leading character faces with dread the fact that his life is passing by rapidly. He sees that opportunities which once appeared so promising have been missed, never to return. "Time is the enemy of us all," he declares.

"Enemy" may be too strong a word, but at the very best, time is a challenging adversary to be dealt with one way or another. Nowhere is this reality more compelling than in the life of a truly ambitious careerist. For these people, failure to recognize that time is inescapably a limited, fixed resource constitutes an ever-present threat to success.

At birth, you and I were given about 23,000 days until we reach normal retirement at age of 65. We have exactly 168 hours per week – 8,736 hours per year – to accomplish all we will ever get done. No more, no less.

It is well to keep in mind what C.S. Lewis, the British academic and writer, had to say on that score: "The future is something which everyone reaches at the rate of 60 minutes an hour, whatever he does, whoever he is."

The more acute your sense of the passage of time, the greater your chances of success.

John A. Georges, chairman of International Paper Company, put the matter in these terms in a recent speech: "Every day, in every way, each of us uses up some of our potential."

In his book, HOW TO GET CONTROL OF YOUR TIME AND YOUR LIFE, Alan Lakein puts it on the line: "Time is life. It is irreversible and irreplaceable. To waste your time is to waste your life, but to master your time is to master your life and make the most of it."

There are carloads of books and tapes filled with good ideas on time management. You should read one or two of these. But be careful; you can get mired down in a swamp of how-to-do-it advice.

This then becomes a great waste of time and an easy excuse for replacing urgency with procrastination.

The idea of time is truly awesome, but the *concept* of what to do about it is simple if we discipline ourselves to act.

In reality, the use of time does not represent a few big, dramatic, earth-shattering, fork-in-the road decisions.

The way we use our time is determined by hundreds of choices – most of them little decisions – we make each day, week, month and year about what to do and when to do it.

The key for meaningful action to maximize your utilization of time (i.e. success) is to live by this simple formula.

DO

DO IT

DO IT NOW

"Do" means be active, always moving to accomplish the next step toward one of your goals.

"Do it" means act on specifics that relate to the goal on which you are working. Avoid vague generalities.

"Do it now" means act now on a specific step. If common sense says use controlled procrastination on one project, move on *now* to act on another goal.

DO SOMETHING SPECIFIC NOW.

Common sense tells us to recognize that time can be an alluring seductress. It seems to offer a bed of comfort to be enjoyed at one's own pace with no due-bill demanding to be paid sooner or later. Know time for what it is, a perishable resource with a finite shelf life. Use it or lose it!

USE THE POSITIVE POWER OF NEGATIVE THINKING

Positive thinking is widely recognized as a critical ingredient for career success. But fast-track achievers – those who consistently ring the bell – have learned that this powerful force must be leavened with the proper amount of negative thinking for top-notch performance, day-in and day-out.

It is just common sense to recognize there can be positive power in negative thinking.

The wise careerist will believe in his heart of hearts that his project – and his career – will be successful. He will be motivated by high expectations, and he will work as hard as possible to see that his goals are attained. At the same time, he will develop alternate plans based on "what if things don't work out?" He will develop what the schools of business call "worst case scenarios." In other words, while he is visualizing success and working toward stretch goals of "the best that can be expected," he will define the other end of the spectrum, which is the maximum exposure to loss.

Negative thinking can be used to lower expectations others may have for your performance.

My baptism into this strategy came early when I observed my first corporate boss, Dick Meredith, deftly advance his career through the use of this powerful force.

Dick was the personnel director and chief labor negotiator for a major forest products manufacturer in Arkansas. As the season for labor negotiations neared, his complexion would take on a sallow hue. We could see his shoulders slump. He complained that he could not sleep and that his health appeared to be failing. He became a walking portrait of worry and depression.

With master strokes, he painted the direst of outlooks. A strike – probably long and costly – was nearly as certain as day following night. A catastrophe could be averted only through the highest of skills and the hardest of efforts, namely his.

153

His boss was by no means gullible. He knew what Dick was doing and Dick knew he knew. Nevertheless, Dick's strategy worked because he was practiced at the art of using negative thinking to achieve his goals. Moreover, who was going to be foolish enough to suggest that the unions would cave in, so management could relax? What if the workers did go out on strike? In retrospect, the optimistic ones would look naive at best.

Three things always resulted from Dick's negative scenarios. One, an apprehensive senior management group was more than willing to put authority and responsibility for the negotiations in his hands. (Who wanted to be tarred with that sticky brush?) Two, they were ready to approve a more generous settlement. (After all, they understood from Dick that a strike would cause havoc to rain down on the company.) Three, he was a real hero when the company got by without a strike for another year, which it usually did, by offering generous settlements. (Hadn't he warned that the day would be saved only by the most heroic of efforts?)

Negative thinking is necessary to complete the circle of good planning.

Let's suppose you are placed in charge of the annual company picnic. You make your checklist of the arrangements including supplies and logistics. You go into your boss to report – with considerable pride – that everything is in order.

He leans back in his chair and studies your report.

"This looks great, Charlie," he says.

However, before your satisfaction gets off the ground he adds a "but."

"Charlie, what happens if it starts raining that morning? What arrangements have you made if someone gets sick, say has a heart attack? What if the mosquitoes are really bad by the lake that day?"

His list of "what ifs" goes on for awhile.

That is negative thinking for sure, but who can say it doesn't make sense to apply this discipline to all plans.

I call it "Titanic Planning."

Some six years before the Titanic (the infamous ocean liner) went down, Captain Edward J. Smith, its future commander, declared, "I cannot imagine any condition which would cause a ship to founder …modern ship building has gone beyond that."

Apparently harboring some negative thoughts, a passenger is reported to have asked a deckhand, "Is this ship really unsinkable?" In the ultimate burst of positive thinking, the young man replied, "Madam, God himself could not sink this ship."

At 20 minutes to midnight on Sunday, April 14, 1912, the Titanic, on her first Trans-Atlantic voyage, struck an iceberg while steaming 300 miles off the coast of Newfoundland. Mortally wounded by a 300-foot gash in its hull, the ship, thought to be unsinkable, went to the bottom in about two and one-half hours.

Too bad someone hadn't leavened all that blind confidence with a little negative thinking. There was room for less than half of the approximately 2,200 passengers in the lifeboats the positive thinking builders had provided. Only 705 people, mostly women and children, survived the icy waters of the North Atlantic.

The lesson here is very clear. The owners might not have sold as many tickets on that first trip if they had made a public case about the negative possibilities. However, it is equally obvious that they would have been ahead of the game in the long run if they had done some quiet behind-the-scenes planning for the negatives.

Winners in all walks of life make a practice of spending some time thinking about the negatives in order to improve their performance.

Betsy King, one of the greatest performers the world of women's golf has ever produced, says she is apt to spend more time thinking about a bad shot she made than the good ones.

In THE NAME OF THE GAME IS LIFE, a book in which 13 of life's winners reflect on the lessons of athletics that helped make them successful, King is quoted as saying:

"The easiest way to change a bad habit is to think about it while you practice at the driving range. Then think constantly during the match about what you learned to do to correct the error. Keep at it until doing it right becomes natural. If you don't recognize your problems and think about them, how can you correct what you have been doing wrong?"

However, those men and women who recognize the "positive power of negative thinking" are still in the minority.

Many managers get so carried away with trying to put a positive face on every event – no matter how big a disaster it may be – that they come off looking stupid or worse.

Exxon wasn't ready when one of its tankers, the "Exxon Valdez," spilled 11 million gallons of oil in Alaska's Prince William Sound.

A company spokesman assured the world that Exxon had preplanned "to ensure rapid and effective response to any oil spill emergency," but went on to say, "No, we never envisioned anything like this."

Fortune magazine declared that the company's response showed "confusion and lack of preparation."

Lawrence Rawls, CEO of Exxon at that time, was roundly criticized for what, in effect, was his company's failure to think negatively. Later he advised other corporate executives: "You'd better pre-think which way you are going to jump...before you have any kind of problem...even though it's hard to force yourself to think in terms of a chemical plant blowing up or spilling oil in Prince William Sound."

Admittedly, the very thought that there is value in negative thinking flies in the face of the blizzard of popular career and management literature that so often seems to say, "Think positively and all will end well."

Mention of the positive power of negative thinking is not to be found in the stacks of "how-to-be-successful-in-10-easy-lessons" volumes that grace the shelves of bookstores.

But experience teaches those who listen that there are more values than a bit of irony and a hearty chuckle to be found in Murphy's Laws.

How do these laws square with your experience?

- Everything takes longer to accomplish than we first imagine.
- Everything is more difficult to accomplish than we anticipate.
- Everything costs more than we expect.
- If anything can go wrong, it will.

Successful managers make their positive plans and put them through "The Titanic" test. They ask six basic questions about any major project.

- What can go wrong?
- What must I do to prevent my project from jumping track?
- If, despite my best efforts, the project does derail, what will I do to straighten out the wreckage and minimize my losses?
- Is the potential reward worth the risk?
- If I lose, how will it affect my other enterprises?
- Can I afford those results?

Another term for negative thinking is *realistic thinking* about the way the world really works. It is a matter of insisting on facts and resisting the allure of promises of success gained too easily.

Don't expect that applying the positive force of negative thinking will be an easy row to hoe. In fact, negative thinking, no matter how sound it may be, is usually downright unpopular.

The president of a Fortune 500 consumer goods company found himself in a shoot-out with his chairman when he tried to introduce the reality of negative thinking at the company's annual management meeting.

The chairman had opened the meeting by singing a stirring rendition of "You gotta accentuate the positive, eliminate the negative." The rainbow was bright and the pot of gold surely was to be found at the end of it.

When the president's turn came to speak, he warned of thunder-clouds on the horizon. He urged each division manager to develop a "Plan B" in the event it did rain. Have a plan, he said, for cutting expenses, delaying capital expenditures, and putting a freeze on new hires.

Enraged by such negative thinking, the chairman closed his mind to all doubts and redoubled his efforts to make his plan work. He also set out that day to fire the president.

A few months later, when the thunderstorms of a sick economy hit, it was the chairman who was ousted by the board of directors. They named the president to replace him.

He put "Plan B" into effect but it was too little, too late. The company and its shareholders suffered.

Negative thinking is strong medicine. Therefore, the prescription for it requires appropriate warnings on the label: "Properly administered, negative thinking will improve your performance. However, it must be taken with care and discretion. Too strong a dose, taken too frequently, may cause disorientation, defeatism, paralysis and other counterproductive behavior. Negative thinking may be habit-forming."

Your ability to effectively administer the powerful force of negative thinking is a sure sign you are on the track to success. It will be a bumpy ride from time to time, but if skillfully negotiated, the trip will pay off for you and your organization.

After all, it is simply a matter of always having an umbrella within easy reach in case it rains. Successful careerists know that it does rain sooner or later, and they don't let themselves get wet unnecessarily.

EXORCISE THE FEAR OF CHANGE

Change is certain and constant. Benjamin Franklin would have been wise to add "change" to his adage that "death and taxes are the only certainties in life."

All of us are inundated every day, at an incredible rate, by change – new associations, new ways to do things, new expectations, and new information. The total of all knowledge doubles every five years. *The Futurist* magazine projects that 75 percent of all current workers will need retraining by the year 2000; today's high school graduates will have to be prepared to change jobs or careers at least 10 times in their lifetime.

There is a direct correlation between the way we handle change and our career success.

We can resist change – deny its existence, keep on doing things in the same old way because "that's the way we've always done them." Then, we will be buried with other relics of the past, done in by what Alvin Toffler called, "Future Shock."

We can merely accept change and go along with the world it produces for us. If so, we will dance on cue to whatever tune the fiddler chooses to play.

Or, we can recognize that change is inevitable and embrace it. We can become agents of change so we have a hand in shaping the environment in which we live and in determining our own success.

Common sense tells us, if we are ambitious, that we must initiate and manage change. The alternative is obvious: be content to remain with the old and familiar, accepting the idea that the comfort of a known and static environment is worth being left behind while our competitors roll forward.

Peter Drucker, the chief management guru, declares, "...success always means organizing for the abandonment of what has already been achieved. There is no more difficult challenge."

This means to try new and unfamiliar ideas, untested ground, unthinkable thoughts. It is frequently uncomfortable, often dangerous, but always exciting territory. Like it or not, that is where the gold is to be found.

Machiavelli wrote in *The Prince* in the early 1500s: "There is nothing more difficult to take in hand, more perilous to conduct, or more uncertain in its success, than to take the lead in the introduction of a new order of things, because the innovator has for enemies all those who have done well under the old conditions, and lukewarm defenders in those who may do well under the new."

Accept the idea that change is frightening. Our fear grows out of the uncertainties and ambiguities that change always produces. Being an agent of change and a beneficiary requires flexibility and imagination, as well as courage. Dealing with change requires tolerance for the unknown.

Change and its handmaiden ambiguity go against the grain of human nature; many people simply can't tolerate that condition. They want everything in order and ready answers for all questions. Unfortunately, that is not the nature of change.

The successful careerists will recognize that uncertainties offer the opportunity for answers and for leadership. Confident in their abilities and the future, they will seize the moment.

No one ever said it would be easy.

But common sense tells us that we have no choice because change – at an ever increasing pace – is a sure bet. We also know that unless we change ourselves and bring about change in the organization where we live and work, there can be no progress.

LEARN TO PLAY POLITICS

Like it or not, it is just common sense to recognize that politics exist in the workplace. Furthermore, there is no escaping the fact that organizational politics have a powerful influence on your career.

Therefore, it is important to learn how to play the game.

Most of us are reluctant to admit the presence of politics in our careers. It is somewhat like having a horse thief in the family tree. Everybody knows he's there, but nobody wants to acknowledge his presence. When we do, it is with a lot of finger pointing.

Politics exist in all organizations to one degree or another. This has been true ever since man entered into his first organizational relationships to hunt for game. It will always be true when as many as two people get together to accomplish a task.

"What we are talking about is the lifeblood of a company. It is how people influence each other outside official channels, because no business operates the way the organization chart says it does," says Val Arnold, a personnel consultant. He believes if it did, "nothing would get done."

Eight out of 10 readers of *Weekend* magazine, who participated in a survey about politics on the job, recognized it is necessary to "play the game." (Only slightly more than one-third think they play it well.)

Nearly one-half felt that "getting along with the boss" counts most. Just under one out of three thought excellent work is the first requirement.

However, there is a significant split between career *winners* and *losers* when it comes to opinions about the importance of politics.

Weekend reports, "47 percent of career *winners* say doing excellent work counts most; only 26 percent rank getting along with the boss as the key to getting ahead."

Losers reverse this view. Almost 60 percent say that getting along with the boss counts most. Only one out of five recognize excellent work as the most important factor.

The issue is not whether politics exist in the workplace, it is how politics are used.

Politics come in two varieties.

There are "good" politics, which are the power and lubrication that keep the organization running. There are "bad" politics, which seek to manipulate the organization toward the service of special, selfish interests.

Unfortunately, the popular notion is that politics mean deviousness, manipulation and compromise. In other words, "bad" politics.

But politics can be healthy and constructive when we recognize that to lead, manage and get things done through other people (i.e. the classic role of a manager) we must be able to define issues, have a vision of the future, develop constituencies and form alliances. That's "good" politics in the true definition of the term, which is: "the art of adjusting and ordering relationships between individuals and groups...activities concerned with governing or with influencing or winning and holding control (of an organization)...the relations between leaders and non-leaders in any social group."

Playing "bad" politics is frequently very tempting because it promises to yield quick and easy results. That may be the case, but there is usually a price to pay at some point. Long-term careers are seldom built when there is a heavy reliance on "bad" politics. Besides, the kind of manipulation called for is likely to be a harder task than playing it straight. Certainly, it involves more risks.

"Good" politics, on the other hand, offer more sound results in terms of career success, pride and satisfaction. This is because "good politics" depend on doing a good job, getting credit for it and developing positive relationships with several constituencies.

You will most often come to the heart of politics in the matter of choosing sides. The reality is there are factions in all organizations. Sooner or later, you will have to decide which team you will join and support. This is touchy, but necessary business. Loners don't get far in organizations.

It is a mistake to pick a side simply because it appears to be winning the battle at hand, without taking into account who is likely to win the war. Those who bend with every new wind are not going to build status with any faction. Those who jump from one side to the other without any convictions other than expediency are very apt to outsmart themselves one day and end up with the short end of the stick. Those who live by "bad" politics should not be surprised if they die in the same way.

It is better to play it straight for what one believes to be the good of the organization. This means supporting the side whose ideas and policies look to be the soundest for the long term, and with which one feels the strongest bond. That team will probably win in the end. But as one careerist said, "Even if they lose out…they might wind up at a different company in better jobs – and take their loyal supporters along."

NOTHING HAPPENS UNTIL YOU SELL YOURSELF

A well-worn adage advises us that we have only to invent a better mousetrap, and the world will beat a path to our door, bearing recognition and riches.

Forget it!

That may have been good advice when Ralph Waldo Emerson recommended it in the mid-1880s, but it falls short for the truly ambitious careerist who is out to win in the clutter and clamor of today's intensely competitive world.

If you are content simply to build a better mousetrap and sit back waiting for the buyers to come calling, you are likely to end up with a shelfful of unused and wasted assets.

The harsh reality is there are plenty of smart people capable of providing profitable ideas, products and services. There is a great degree of parity among men and women turning out quality mousetraps.

The fact that you have invented the best mousetrap is only the first step toward success. Until those people empowered to make buying decisions are aware of your mousetraps and decide to choose you as the supplier, you will be spinning your wheels waiting vainly for success.

This reality applies to men and women who work in the hierarchy of organizations every bit as forcefully as it does to those who operate retail stores and professional practices.

Nothing happens until you sell yourself.

There is no question that self-promotion is a very delicate matter with which few people are comfortable. It is a difficult subject to discuss objectively. The idea generates a knee-jerk reaction: "I'd be too embarrassed to promote myself, even if I wanted to. Besides, my work speaks for itself."

Sometimes our hesitancy grows out of peer pressure. "Don't raise your own flag too high above the rest of us," the group says. "We'll all be put on the spot. We may have to perform up to a higher standard."

This is a counterproductive attitude which serves no good, except for those who are willing to lag behind or who want to protect their flanks by holding others back.

Overt braggarts are certainly pains in the neck. Braggadocio will usually backfire. On the other hand, doing a good job consistently and letting the world know about it in an appropriate way is an essential to success.

This means thinking objectively of yourself and what you have to offer. Remember the point made earlier: you are a product – a valuable one – to be sold.

Here are some suggestions that may help you promote your career.

First, be absolutely sure that your performance deserves recognition and reward. You are programmed for failure if you try to take credit for more than you have done. The facts must sustain the claim.

The next step seems to be painfully obvious, but many people overlook it. Be sure your boss knows what you are accomplishing. He may be taking you for granted. Submit progress reports in writing. Remember "carbon copies." Use them often, but judiciously. It is productive to let the rest of the organization in on your story.

"Talk about (your) accomplishments in a proud way," advises Celia D. Crossely, a career strategist. "Try to use the same tone you would use in announcing a wedding or the birth of a new baby."

Be visible throughout the organization. Seek opportunities to work with other departments. Make contacts and friends. Let them know what you do. Volunteer to lead the interdepartmental task forces.

If your organization has a communications or public relations office, get to know the people who work there. Help them. If you demonstrate you are a willing and knowledgeable source, they are more likely to publicize the work you and your team are doing.

Get active in trade associations, civic clubs and public service activities. With the organization's permission, make speeches and write articles for the trade press and general news media. Everybody wins. Your employer basks in the sunlight of your achievements. You gain visibility and contacts. You polish your skills and talents.

If you have done a job alone, don't hesitate to accept the credit. Be just as quick to share the accolades when there is a team effort. Credits accrue for wise leadership, too, when you share the accolades.

If you are still reluctant to promote your wares, ask yourself these questions.

If I have something of benefit to provide, don't I owe it to those who depend on me, to my employer and to myself to let the rest of the world know about it? Am I on a self-centered ego trip if I sit back and expect the world to beat a path to my door? Whose interests are being served?

How many mice will I help eliminate if I build a better mousetrap, but nobody buys one because they don't know about its value?

EXPECT SOME HARD KNOCKS AND DETOURS
ALONG THE CAREER PATH

There is no such thing as a career – or even a single job – without some setbacks and disappointments. You may be passed over for promotion or denied a raise. Boredom from time to time is par for the course. You will get fed up sometimes in the best of situations.

Expect these unpleasant conditions and be prepared to deal with them. The following chapters should help you along the way.

ATTA-BOYS ARE HARDER TO COME BY UP THE LADDER

Go ahead. Admit it.

You got in a funk now and then when your teachers or coaches failed to give you a pat on the back for a job well done. Expect that reaction to occur on the job.

That's okay, just so long as it doesn't happen too often and you are not out of sorts for too long. Whatever you do, don't let it show. Learn to manage this all-too human emotion.

Everyone wants and needs to be stroked, to be praised for doing a good job. This need never goes away entirely, no matter where one is on the career ladder. "Atta-boys" are always important to self-esteem and effectiveness.

"The deepest principle of human nature is the craving to be appreciated," according to William James, the great American psychologist.

"Appreciation" ranked second, just behind money and one place ahead of pride, among the most desired rewards for work, according to a survey of members of the Institute of Industrial Engineers.

However, the truly ambitious careerist who is willing to pay the price for success has to learn a lesson early on about the way the world works when it comes to compliments. The reality is that the sources of stroking change and the flow diminishes as one rises to greater responsibilities.

The reality is that "atta-boys" are harder to come by the higher you rise in the organization.

Your ability to handle this condition will play a key role in how far and how fast you climb in your career. If you are too eager and can't control the urge for compliments, you will too often play to the grandstands for applause instead of keeping your focus on the objectives. Ultimately, you may fall victim to your insecurities, which are the root of the problem.

Why is it the more success you achieve, the less overt, sincere stroking you are likely to receive on the job?

For one thing, it stands to reason that the higher you climb up the pyramid, the fewer people there are in positions to pay you compliments.

Subordinates are reluctant to tell you that you did a good job for fear they will be seen as "polishing the apple." Moreover, they are apt to think you don't need encouragement. After all, you are the boss. Even if your subordinates do pay you a compliment, can you be absolutely sure they are NOT putting a shine on the apple?

The higher you rise, the more likely you are to find bosses who are so rushed they will not have time to pass out thank-you notes. They may be praising you in their own way. Or they don't think it is important "at your level."

You may have a boss like Lou Gerstner, CEO of IBM, a man rated as one of the toughest and more effective executives in America.

Working with Gerstner in all sorts of situations when he headed up the worldwide travel-related services business at American Express, I came to admire him as a superb piece of management machinery. He seems to function on a plane somewhat removed from most of his colleagues. He is self-contained, like a fine watch with a lifetime battery. He doesn't appear to want or expect approval from others. He is all business. Charming when he wants to be, when dealing with managers, his attitude is, "Look, we are here to do a job. We get paid well for delivering results that should be expected from mature professionals. I don't have to go around stroking everyone. That's for kids."

But Gerstner can switch styles in a different setting.

One of his associates says that the man knows how to turn on the motivation when he is touring a plant. He will stop to visit with a worker on the production line, inquire about his job and pass out a compliment, leaving the employee on cloud nine.

Walking away, he may turn off the beam and conclude that there are too many people on the payroll.

Nearer the top, you may be working for bosses who manage by exception. That is, they only have time to focus on things that are going wrong.

Or the compliments may be there, but because they are in a different form you miss hearing them.

The vice president of corporate communications at an international manufacturing concern was incensed at how little attention his boss, the chairman, paid to his area of responsibility. The young man blew his top at one point when the CEO spent only a few minutes glancing over and approving the annual message to shareholders, which had been written by the vice president.

"He just doesn't care," the young executive told me. "He never has a complimentary thing to say."

With more objectivity, I was able to point out that the chairman had just paid him a very significant compliment. He knew the work would be first class. He didn't have to worry that the message and the writing would be off target. He didn't think it was necessary to say "good work." Besides, he was probably preoccupied with other matters, such as slumping sales, an irate investor with a bundle of shares, or a defecting executive.

Incidentally, my good friend and client had been consistently receiving top salary increases and bonuses for his work.

But those rewards weren't enough. He was letting the primary urge for recognition distract him from his work and his goals.

It takes a lot of maturity and confidence to realize that while the kind of obtuse pat-on-the-back the vice president received is not as obvious and as pleasing to the ego as stand-up recognition at an employee dinner or a mention in the company newsletter, it is ultimately more important.

You are well served when you can expect to receive less overt praise as you get promoted because you will be doing fewer specific, measurable things that can be singled out for recognition.

Some people can't handle that.

Sara Green was a prize-winning salesperson by any measure. She won the president's trophy each year. She was so good that in the infinite wisdom of management, she was moved from her district to the position of general sales manager.

Sara was a flop as a boss, almost from day one.

Instead of the flow of praise from her superiors for her individual triumphs that could be easily quantified, she was instead managing the sales process. She was the one writing the congratulatory memos and making the "you-are-terrific" telephone calls.

Within a year, by her own choice, Sara was back in the field selling. She was willing to trade a higher position in the hierarchy for pats on the back at a lower level. Kudos were more important than power in the organization and opportunities for advancement...even more desirable to her than money.

What can you do about this paradox between the deepest human yearning and the realities of the world of work?

First of all, you should learn to be more the parent and less the child. Leaders realize they have to become more of a *source* of compliments for others than a *receiver* of them.

It is important to understand that the best recognition an organization can give you is to demonstrate faith in your abilities by giving you more responsibilities, and to compensate you fairly when you meet them.

This means you must discipline yourself to turn inward for satisfaction and stroking. You will be a stronger career competitor when you become able to find the greatest source of ego-building satisfaction within yourself.

Careerists who are able to stay the course to successful finishes are the men and women who are primarily self-contained. They know what they can do. The drive to satisfy their own standards is enough to motivate them to achieve.

The only external recognition they need is a growing career with opportunities to take on more and more responsibilities and equitable compensation for what they deliver. But if they don't receive these rewards, the true achievers will survive and prosper on the fuel of their own motivation.

SO YOU ARE FED UP WITH YOUR JOB

So you find you are fed up with your job. You want to make a change.

Well, as the old saying goes, misery loves company. Surveys show that as many as two out of three working Americans are unhappy with their jobs. A study by the *Wall Street Journal* reveals that over half of the people with annual incomes below $50,000 would choose a different profession if they could start over. That figure moves up to three out of four with household incomes of over $100,000.

But before you jump ship, be certain you have good and sound reasons for wanting to make a change. Are you just bored or are you running away from personal problems that will tag along wherever you go?

Are there things you can do to make your present employment more acceptable?

David Ford owned a thriving business. By working extremely hard six and one-half days a week, with never a vacation, he was able to hold down expenses and turn a nice profit for a number of years. But finally the brutal schedule burned him out.

He sold the business for a handsome profit. He moved away from his hometown and invested in another business which failed. He has worked for others for the past several years.

David has never been as happy since he sold his business.

"Looking back on it, " he says, "it was the biggest mistake of my life. All I really needed was a good vacation."

Don't be lulled into believing that the grass will be necessarily greener in another pasture. Or that a new pasture will be a great deal different from the one where you are grazing now.

It is true, as the early-American writer Washington Irving put it: "There is a certain relief in change, even though it be from bad to worse; as I have found in traveling in a stagecoach, it is often a comfort to shift one's position and be bruised in a new place."

Absent the most extreme reasons, do not leave your present job until you have another one firmly secured. If ever it was true that a bird in hand is worth two in the bush, it is when a job is concerned. Remember, it is always easier to get a job when you have one.

Take the time to figure out what you really want to do. What will it take to make you and your loved ones happier?

It is not enough to know what you want to change from. You need to know what you want to change to.

Be specific in these definitions. Don't allow yourself to be driven by a sense of vague malaise to make a change just for the sake of a change. If you can't spell out in writing the valid reasons you want to move to a new job and be equally as specific about what you want to do, don't set the process in motion.

Recognize that you are contemplating a serious and difficult undertaking. Determine that you have the courage to live with the dangers and uncertainties of making a change. There is always some risk to your present situation when you start looking around. What will your present employer think if the word gets around that you are "looking"? At best the whole process is disruptive and can be traumatic for you and your loved ones.

As a sixteenth century British theologian observed, "Change is not made without inconvenience, even from worse to better."

Survey the situation. Be sure there is a market for the skills you have to offer. Know for certain there are opportunities where you and your family want to live.

If, after giving the matter careful thought, you are convinced you would be better off in a new situation, *go for it.*

It will not be a time for half measures. To vacillate between courting new employers and sitting back in a coy mode, hoping to be courted, will surely breed frustration. Employ the same strategy you used to get your first full-time job. Mount a campaign and invest whatever time and energy are required to reach your objective. Charge full steam ahead.

If you have something to offer that the market wants, you will find a new job. However, count on it taking time. And there may come a point when you decide that by comparison your present situation looks quite attractive. So you may opt to stay put, at least for the time being.

And don't worry about there being a stigma attached to changing jobs. You will find a lot of other people out there shopping for new jobs. The president of the American Association of State Colleges and Universities recently told a group of college seniors that by the age of 40, they could expect that on average they would have held eight different jobs.

In fact, some personnel recruiters argue that your resume will be stronger if it shows movement from job to job so long as the reasons for changing are positive and they are not too frequent.

In any case, if you are constantly unhappy and frustrated because of your work, set out to make a change. Life is too short to do otherwise.

BEING PASSED OVER IS HARD TO ACCEPT

You sincerely believe you are the best qualified among the candidates for the promotion to manager of your department. You are convinced you deserve it. All of your friends reassure you.

Wham! The rug is pulled out from under you, suddenly and without ceremony. The position you want so badly goes to someone else.

You are convinced all the world will see that the organization doesn't think you are as good as the other person. Your ego is trampled. You are mad and disappointed. You want to march in, tell the boss where to go and leave the place.

But hold on. Apply a little common sense before you go off the deep end.

Force your chin up. Congratulate the winner as soon as possible. This may be painful at the time, but it actually will help you regain your balance. Moreover, it will strengthen your position.

This is a dangerous time for you. Simmer awhile before you act. Brood and grieve a little in private if it makes you feel better. But reject bitterness. It is pure poison. After you have been through this process, review the situation.

Being passed over may be a blessing, although if it is, it appears to be quite well disguised. If you get passed over early in your career, you may be able to gain a more realistic view of where you are, where you want to go and what you have to do to get there.

It is virtually impossible for any of us to be objective about ourselves, but this is certainly a time to try. Focus on the critical questions about what happened and why. Tell yourself the truth. Have your performance on your present job and your preparation for the next step been as good as they could have been? Are you better qualified than the competitor who got the promotion? What might you have done to improve your chances to win the position?

Did you miss some signals from your boss, telling you to improve your performance? Were there any authentic indicators saying you were a candidate for promotion? Or have you been engaged in wishful thinking?

Look beyond your ego. Sure, your feelings have been bruised. No need to be ashamed of that. But has all of this really been damaging to your long-term career goals?

Having sorted through these types of questions, it is appropriate to have a serious discussion with your boss or whomever made the decision to give the assignment to someone else.

Don't beat around the bush. Tell the boss you are sorely disappointed to have missed the opportunity. Assure him there is no bitterness or resentment; pledge 100 percent allegiance to the team. Point out, however, that you are concerned about what has happened and what it may mean for your future.

Be tactful, but remember, you are searching for answers to the key question: Why not me?

You need to know if you were a serious candidate. What did the job require that you were short on? Will there be other chances to win promotions? What can you do to improve your qualifications for advancement?

At this point, you will have to listen as you have never listened before to what is said, as well as what is implied between the lines. Be aware that you will be strongly inclined to hear the best side of the story. Resist that urge. You are at a critical checkpoint in your career where you need facts. And don't forget, it is the most natural thing in the world for the boss to try to soften the message. Unless he has a cordial dislike for you, or you are a complete dud, he will probably want to avoid any criticisms, lest you be further deflated. Most managers find it difficult to give frank evaluations, so he may be "going around the barn" to tell you about your shortcomings. Besides, if you have been doing an adequate job in your present slot, he will want to keep you around. Or he simply may be testing you for a bigger assignment.

Now you are ready to get to the bottom line. Review the situation. What are the facts? Have you been treated fairly? Were there legitimate reasons you were passed over? Now that you are past the initial shock, do you care enough, do you have enough energy and ambition to take the necessary action to win the next time or to find a more rewarding situation elsewhere? What acceptable alternatives are in view? Do you have a reasonably secure future in the organization? Can you be happy where you are?

The *truly ambitious* careerist may want to seriously consider this suggestion from a consultant who advises managers about career moves: "Prepare to leave if you get passed over once. Leave if you get passed over twice."

WHO IS TO BLAME IF YOU GET PASSED OVER?

Who or what is to blame if you are not getting the promotion you want and think you deserve?

Many factors, in various combinations, can be the cause from one situation to another, but one thing is 90 percent certain. You, yourself, are the key factor in almost every case. Like it or not, you and you alone – your abilities, your attitude and personality, the level of your ambition, all things you can control – must take most of the credit or the blame for the rate of progress in your career.

There is valuable insight in Shakespeare's "Julius Caesar." Cassius, ever the realist, is advising Brutus, a conscientious patriot and prideful man, as they consider their ambitions for bigger and better things:

"The fault, dear Brutus, is not in our stars, but in ourselves, that we are underlings."

Let's examine the common sense truth behind some of the more frequent reasons (or excuses, as the case may be) given to explain why people are not promoted.

You fail to win the promotion because you are not qualified to take on the bigger new responsibilities.

Basically, two things can be happening here. In either case, you have to accept the major part of the responsibility.

One is you have the potential to learn the new responsibilities, but you haven't done so. Hopefully, your employer has a training program. If so, get enrolled without further delay. If there is no such program, it is up to you to find a way to learn how to handle the bigger job. Study and practice on your own time. Continue to be successful on the job at hand. Be patient, but persistent. Convince your boss you want the promotion and that you can handle it.

The other condition is the job you covet is simply beyond your capacity to learn. You must accept the fact that you, like every other human being, have limits to your capabilities. But recognize you are in control of what happens. You have at least two options: be content where you are, or strike out in a different and more realistic direction where your ceiling is higher.

You can't be promoted because there is no one to take over your present responsibilities.

Your employer, if the company is well managed, should have a training program in place to provide lines of succession for all key positions. If your place of work is not so prepared, you still can't place the blame for your lack of promotion on someone or something else.

If you are stymied for lack of a replacement, it is up to you to make certain that at least one person is ready to step in and take your place. Pick out a likely candidate and train him or her. Make sure your shoes can be filled.

"They" don't know what you have been doing and how much you can do; how ready you are for promotion. You are not appreciated.

It is often said, "There is no limit to the good a man can do, if he doesn't care who gets the credit." That is a laudable ideal, but unfortunately it doesn't square with reality when it is applied in the competitive world of work. Egos running amok are to be avoided because they are destructive. It is quite another matter to think of yourself as a product that needs to be sold to advance your career. This means the buyers (i.e. your superiors who make decisions about your career) need to be made fully aware of your good qualities, who you are, and what you can do. You can achieve this condition without playing to the grandstands. Do a good job, be prepared for advancement, and communicate the facts.

You have tried repeatedly to get a promotion. Everything is locked up, nobody is leaving, the business is stagnant. There is no room to grow.

You are still the key. If you are certain this is the situation, your career issue is more clearly defined than in most instances. You can accept that you are stuck. Then there are two things you can do. Consider the pluses in your current job. There are always some benefits. Will they continue at least as they are? Are there some personal considerations dictating that you stay where you are for now? (Look twice to be sure they are not being used as convenient excuses for inaction.) Is the price you are paying to live on a plateau below what you believe to be your potential, affordable and worth the benefits? If so, you can stay put and hope for things to get better. If your ambitions and frustrations are burning you up inside, make a move to another organization where you will have opportunities to advance.

The first step toward getting promoted is to understand that the credit or the blame for your career and where it goes is strictly yours. You are in command.

HOW TO GO FOR A RAISE

No one likes to ask for a raise.

It can be a traumatic experience. Who likes to ask for recognition? It is much better for rewards to come unsolicited from someone else.

Although you hope it never happens, there are situations when it makes common sense to say to the boss, "I believe I am worth more to this organization than I am being paid. I would appreciate a raise."

The key word is *worth*.

Never, never, never try to make a case for a raise in pay on the basis of *need*. Organizations can't stay in business for very long by paying people what they need to live on. Organizations can survive only by paying people what they contribute to the bottom line of results.

You are probably justified in asking for a raise when one or more of the following conditions exists.

- You can prove you are making a contribution toward your employer's goals above and beyond what is expected from your position.

- You have been filling a more demanding position, which usually pays more money, for a considerable time, without an increase.

- You haven't had a raise in an unreasonable period of time, while the paychecks of others within your organization and in your market have been getting fatter.

- You have an offer from another employer for more money. You prefer to stay where you are, but you are prepared to leave.

Before you rush off to ask for that raise, you should face the cold fact that one of three things can happen if you take this step. One, you may get the extra money, and all will be well for a time. Two, you may find out you are not nearly as valuable as you thought you were, and that your future is limited to your present position and income. Or, three, you could lose your job when you cause the boss to focus on your value in terms of hard cash.

Do your homework before you ask for more money; be prepared to make a persuasive presentation of your case.

Find out how your compensation compares to other jobs in the company and what other employers are paying for similar responsibilities and experience. Be realistic about what is the fair market value for your talents. You could find out you are already earning top dollar.

Get a reading on how your fellow employees and your boss rate your performance. If you don't get a reasonably good report, you need to rethink your plan to ask for more compensation.

Remember, you are actually making a sales presentation of a product (your service to the organization) to a buyer (your boss) who has a limited budget from which to buy answers to a number of highly competitive needs.

Get directly to the point when you meet with your boss.

Review your contributions, being as specific as possible in such terms as savings, increased productivity, growth in sales. If you are factual and your boss is fair-minded, this should establish a basis of general agreement as to your value.

Underscore your loyalty and longtime commitment to the organization. Suggest your potential for even greater contributions based on demonstrated performance.

Present hard data to prove you are not paid up to scale.

Be prepared to define a range of increase you think is fair, if you are asked to do so. Do not demand.

Be ready to discuss the pros and cons of your performance. It is a rare boss who is not a bit annoyed that you have had to ask, either because he has allowed you to lose touch with reality or because he has failed to recognize your worth and frustration. So don't be surprised at some initial backlash. Accept both praise and criticism with equanimity. Be ready to work out a compromise.

It is unlikely you will get an answer on the spot...unless it is a resounding negative. Demonstrate your maturity by "keeping your cool;" leave the door open for a positive answer or at least further negotiations.

If it is "no," buckle down, do a better job and prepare for another chance. Or leave for a more rewarding environment. Prepare yourself an appropriate response however and whenever you get a raise.

DON'T SHOOT YOURSELF IN THE FOOT WHEN YOU ACCEPT A RAISE

One would think that accepting a raise in pay in a positive way would be as easy as falling off a log. But strangely enough, a lot of people end up shooting themselves in the foot at this crucial time.

Since raises rarely come as surprises, there is no excuse for not being prepared to respond in ways that maximize the situation and pave the way for the next increase.

This means knowing in advance what you will do in each of the two most likely scenarios: the increase in money is in line with what you think you deserve; or you are disappointed because you don't get what you expect.

The first step toward being prepared is to be well informed as to the "going rate." It is the rare employer who doesn't establish a pattern for raises in a given period of time. Raises may be equal to increases in the cost of living, or match the cost of living plus a percentage based on company results. Or there may be a freeze on. Don't expect to be very far outside the norm, unless you have done a truly outstanding job.

Be realistic. Can your employer actually afford to pass out a raise? If so, how much? How much of an increase have you earned?

If you get a raise in the medium range express your appreciation. If you get a very generous raise, be sure your boss knows that you understand and sincerely appreciate that you have been singled out for recognition. Make a verbal commitment to justify the confidence being shown in you.

Never appear to take a raise for granted; however, avoid going overboard in either case. Keep in mind that you earned what you are getting. Your compensation is the price the organization pays for what you deliver. It must never be treated as a gift from a benevolent employer. When the "thank you" is overdone, more than one boss has been led to wonder if he overpaid an employee. Besides an effusive response tends to put the matter on a personal basis, rather than keeping it strictly business, and that is the last thing you want to happen.

What if the raise is below the going rate that others have received for comparable performance and under your expectation? Put on your best poker face. Do not react immediately. As difficult as it may be, say "thank you," but keep it short and subdued. Set out to uncover the reason for the shortfall. If you can make a case that you deserve more, based on your contribution to the company, go back and review the situation with your boss. Be prepared to present the reasons you should be paid more money.

Whatever you do, don't make the mistake that Jim Mullins did.

This otherwise bright young person got off on the wrong foot as the time approached for his annual performance review. In fact, 10 months to the day after he had received a hefty increase, he wrote his boss, Milton Norman, the first of a series of notes reminding him that it was time to think about the amount of his raise. Milton was very annoyed, because to start with, the company's performance was something less than satisfactory. Costs were being cut on every corner. He had assumed Jim knew the situation. Moreover, his own raise had been delayed. When it came, the amount was below his expectations.

Nevertheless, Milton saw a lot of potential in Jim, so he went out on a limb to get approval for an increase of five percent for him, while the standard pay raise was four percent.

When the division chief finally approved an out-of-the-pattern increase for Jim, Milton thought his associate would be happy and appreciative. He looked forward to sharing the information with the young man. However, Milton's enthusiasm turned to outrage at Jim's response.

"That is not acceptable," Jim declared hotly. "Other people are getting more and I deserve a bigger increase. Seven percent will hardly cover the increase in my costs of living since the baby came and we moved into our new home."

Needless to say, their meeting ended on a sour note. But things were to get worse within a few days when Jim hand delivered what has to be ranked as an all-time classic example of what not to do.

"Milton," he wrote, "I learned a couple of things today that I found most distressing. The first is that Joan was promoted again in April, barely 15 months after her previous promotion. Second, she received a 10 percent raise with the promise of a review in a year.

"What I would like to know is:

"Why should I be satisfied with a five percent raise while Kevin gets eight percent? It appears that the cap you've described only applies to me.

"Why is it that you are more interested in the careers of Kevin and Betty than you are in mine? You spend more time with each of them in a day than you do with me in a month.

He concluded by charging, "It is grossly unfair that other managers get annual raises eight percent and higher…and others in my department also regularly get higher and more frequent raises than me.

"I have done more than anyone else in the department to make you look good in the eyes of other senior managers. I think some recognition by you is long overdue.

"Milton, I am one very unhappy camper, and have been for a long time. Learning about Kevin's second promotion was the last straw. I would strongly urge you to move up the timetable for asking the vice president to approve a promotion and significant raise for me."

The relationship between Milton and Jim was damaged beyond repair. A curtain of ice separated them. Jim soon left the company under pressure from Milton and the division manager.

Another example of "how not to do it" is provided by Carlton Moore's handling of his first performance review with his new employer.

George Crow, Carlton's boss, had decided to give him a rating of eight plus on a scale of 10 for his outstanding performance. (George was inclined to give him an even higher score, but he knew the human resources department frowned on near-perfect ratings because they felt, "everyone has some areas in which they can improve.") The eight plus rating meant he would receive a nine percent increase in salary, as compared to the maximum 10 percent and the standard six percent.

At the review, George told Carlton of his high rating and proceeded to point out two or three minor areas where he could do an even better job. He was completely shocked when Carlton started to argue that he deserved a higher evaluation and denied he needed improvement. He persisted without really listening to George's compliments and explanation of the scoring.

Finally, in a fit of exasperation, George agreed to raise Carlton's rating to a near-perfect nine plus. Carlton got his superlative rating and a 10 percent increase. However, George recorded the proceedings in Carlton's personnel file, saying he had been overly rigid and defensive. The review stands out like a sore thumb in his file when the personnel people are identifying candidates for promotions.

The best time to start preparing for next year's raise is the day you receive this year's. The first step is to show your smarts in the way you react to the decision of the organization, whether you are pleased or disappointed.

Above all, work hard to prove you deserved the last raise and the ones to come.

HAVE SOME FUN ALONG THE WAY

Such qualities as loyalty, energy, intelligence and hard work are certain to be in any consensus list of what it takes to build a successful career. However, another essential item is generally overlooked. That is having fun on the job.

In fact, most of us are downright ambivalent when it comes to the subject of fun on the job and taking leisure time away from the work. It is easy to argue both sides of the issue.

We grew up with the proverb, "All work and no play makes Jack a dull boy."

Some ambitious careerists adopt a macho point of view. It expresses itself through a sort of masochistic drive to work more hours than the next fellow, never take a vacation, and otherwise reject the idea that work can be fun.

Some companies force their employees to take time off. Others pay lip service to vacations and then impose a guilt trip on those who get away.

Now the environment seems to be changing. Even the Japanese, notorious workaholics, are discovering there are other things to do after the sun goes down than work.

John Neulinger, author of THE PSYCHOLOGY OF LEISURE and professor emeritus of psychology at City College of New York, states flatly, "Those not interested in doing anything but work are not likely to be CEOs."

Reporting on Dr. Neulinger's work, *Business Week* magazine says he thinks most Americans do not spend enough time seeking leisure, which is more than just piddling away spare time.

True leisure, Neulinger says, is a state of mind. It comes about when a person engages in an activity that produces satisfaction, control and freedom. It is this state of mind that is so essential to the human psyche. It is what provides the regenerative, therapeutic quality of leisure.

The desired change of pace can be achieved by getting away

from the workplace; it can also be gained by having fun on the job.

Studies show that a sense of humor, in proper dosage, can boost creativity and productivity, as well as take the air out of tense situations.

It can help you land the job you want. One study revealed that 98 percent of over 700 chief executive officers interviewed preferred job candidates who have a sense of humor over those who don't.

It has been proven that people work better and faster in a situation where people laugh a lot.

A clinical psychiatrist at Stanford University has found that a good laugh raises the pulse and blood pressure and releases adrenaline into the system. The lungs expand and the torso muscles expand and contract. After laughter, the blood pressure and heart rate return to normal. Laughter is said to be like jogging in place.

"We are going from a climate where humor was belittled, or considered subversive, to a situation where it is highly prized," according to the director of The Humor Project.

Leaders use humor to communicate goals and motivate their followers.

That's why Sam Walton was willing to put on a hula skirt and dance down Wall Street when Wal-Mart employees met a challenge he had laid down.

It is not necessary to be another Johnny Carson to provoke a rejuvenating laugh or enjoy a joke.

Lighten up. Be willing to laugh at yourself. See and tolerate absurdities on the job. They do exist and they are not necessarily the end of the world. Use humor carefully. Don't laugh at people; laugh with them.

Of course, it helps if you believe as did Noel Coward, an English playwright, that "Work is much more fun than fun."

It all comes down to the advice from one sage observer who said, "Get happiness out of your work or you may never know what happiness is."

Example A of Overview of Qualifications

OVERVIEW
SUSAN POWELL
Qualifications For A Position With
MIDWEST PUBLIC SERVICE COMPANY

Susan Powell has an unusual background of education and experience that can be put to work immediately to help strengthen the award-winning communications program at Midwest Public Service.

Graduate Of University of Warren

Susan Powell will graduate (month and year) from the University of Warren, Oakville, Illinois, with a B.A. Degree in Communications with minors in psychology and history. She earned full academic/leadership scholarships for the four years at the university.

Substantial Experience

Susan Powell has substantial work experience directly related to her chosen profession of communications, as well as experience in sales and business management.

Recognized Leadership

Susan Powell's leadership has been recognized in professional organizations such as the Public Relations Society Student Society of America and the Northern Illinois Professional Communicators' Academy. Programs executed by the student public relations society under her leadership have been honored by two business organizations. She has also been elected to positions of leadership by the student body and Faculty Council.

Demonstrated Work Ethic

Susan Powell is a highly-motivated individual with a demonstrated work ethic, plus a commitment to building a successful professional career in communications.

Example B of Overview of Qualifications

OVERVIEW

Qualifications Of
SUSAN POWELL

For A Position With
MIDWEST PUBLIC SERVICE COMPANY

Susan Powell has an unusual background of education and experience that can be put to work immediately to help strengthen the award-winning communications program at Midwest Public Service.

Susan Powell will graduate (month and year) from the University of Warren, Oakville Illinois, with a B.A. Degree in Communications with minors in psychology and history. She earned full academic/leadership scholarships for the four years at the university.

Susan Powell has substantial work experience directly related to her chosen profession of communications, as well as experience in sales and business management.

Susan Powell's leadership has been recognized in professional organizations such as the Public Relations Society Student Society of America and the Northern Illinois Professional Communicators' Academy. Programs executed by the student public relations society under her leadership have been honored by two business organizations. She has been elected to positions of leadership by the student body and Faculty Council.

Susan Powell is a highly-motivated individual with a demonstrated work ethic and a commitment to building a successful professional career in communications.

Example of a basic resume:

Susan Powell
1916 Willow Avenue
Valley View, Illinois
Telephone (708) 537-6324; (312) 446-9823
Fax (708) 537-5534

Summary: Candidate for a position in corporate* communications where working experience with both news media and business organizations can be employed for the mutual benefit of my employer and my long-term career opportunities.

Education: University of Warren, Oakville, Illinois. B. A. Degree in Communications with minors in psychology and history. Attended all four years with benefits from full academic/leadership scholarships.

Experience:
• Worked as summer intern in Corporate Communications Department of International Paper Company at Memphis, Tennessee, operating headquarters, summer of 1994. Completed research and outlined scripts for production of video on the company's environmental programs in Arkansas, Tennessee and Mississippi. Participated in writing report on company's scholarship program.
• Worked part-time during junior and senior years at *Oakville Tribune*. Organized the first campus news bureau at the University of Warren to serve *The Tribune* and major wire services.
• Worked part-time freshman and sophomore years as salesperson for an Oakville sporting goods store and as correspondent for hometown newspaper, *The Valley View News*.
• Worked full-time for three summers and part-time for three years during high school at Valley View Pizza Emporium. During final summer and senior year served as shift manager, overseeing all functions and staff of six.

Income earned from working in several part-time jobs enabled me to pay all college expenses not covered by scholarships.

Activities and honors: Charter president of the Public Relations Student Society of America, University of Warren chapter. Public service programs executed by PRSSA chapter recognized by Oakville Chamber of Commerce and the Sales Executives Club of Oakville. Selected by Northern Illinois Professional Communicators' Academy as winner of the Golden Pen Award for excellence in communications. Named in junior and senior years to Campus Leadership Council by vote of student body and university faculty.

(Personal and professional references attached.)

Note to the reader: Your resume can be prepared for positions with other types of organizations such as a communications agency, a not-for-profit, government, or such specific fields as health care or public utilities.

Example of letter seeking contact/informational interview.

Mr. Wayne Collins
Chairman of The Board
Enjob Corporation
123 Main Street
Maintown, Indiana 12345

Dear Mr. Collins:

I need your advice as I am preparing to graduate this spring from The University of Warren and begin my career in business.

Having earned the chief executive officer's position in a company that has a demonstrated record of profitable growth and community service, you have insights into *what it takes to succeed* that would be most helpful to me. I hope you can share a few minutes of your time with me.

I am enclosing an overview of my immediate career objective, my qualifications, as well as a list of topics that I hope to be able to discuss with you.*

My objective at this point is not to interview for a position with Enjob Corporation. It is to secure information that will enable me to execute a marketing program that will result in the job for which I am best suited.

I will telephone your office (set date) to determine when it will be most convenient for you to share no more than 30 minutes of your valuable time with me.

Sincerely yours,

Susan Powell

* *Note to reader:* See section of book dealing with Contact/Informational Interviews.

**Example of letter seeking job interview
with targeted candidate employer.**

Mr. Gerald O'Brien
Senior Vice President-Corporate Communications
Midwest Public Service Company
891 West Third Avenue
Chicago, Illinois 12345

Dear Mr. O'Brien:

Congratulations to you and your associates on the occasion of Midwest Public Service Company being selected by the Communications Society of America as the 1994 recipient of the Coleman Award as the outstanding corporate communicator in the Midwest.

Our communication classes at the University of Warren have frequently used you and your company as case histories of "how it should be done."

I will be graduating in June from the university. As you will see from the attached overview of my qualifications,* *I have an unusual background of both education and working experience* that I believe prepares me to make a contribution from day one to the award-winning communications program at Midwest Public Service.

I would appreciate an opportunity to discuss how my qualifications can be put to work for the benefit of your company. I will call your office (set date) for an appointment.

Thank you for your consideration.

Sincerely yours,

Susan Powell

Note to the reader: You may choose to send basic resumes instead of the overview depending on what you may have learned from your research into the candidate employer's practices.

Example of sales letter to targeted candidate employer.

Mr. John Paul Simpson, Vice President
Allied Manufacturing Company
123 Main Street
Moline, Illinois 12134

Dear Mr. Simpson:

The recently announced expansion of Allied Manufacturing Company will create many communications challenges as you establish your corporate presence in two new communities.

I believe that my background in terms of education and working experience qualify me to help you and your staff deal with these challenges.

I will be graduating in June from the University of Warren with a B.A. degree in Communications with minors in psychology and history. I received full scholarships for four years. My working experience includes a summer internship in corporate communications with International Paper Company, and part-time employment with two newspapers.

I was president of the Public Relations Student Society of America. Our public service programs won recognition by two business groups. The Professional Communicators' Academy of Northern Illinois selected me as 1994 recipient of their Golden Pen Award for excellence in communications. I was also elected to campus leadership positions by a vote of both the student body and the faculty.

May I have an opportunity to discuss with you my qualifications and how I can put them to work for you and Allied Manufacturing Company? I will call your office on (date) for an appointment.

Sincerely yours,

Susan Powell

Example of letter "broadcasting" for interviews beyond targeted candidate employers.

Ms. Ruth Boone
Vice President-Corporate Communications
Olympiad Aircraft Corporation
Highland Industrial Park
Highland, Wisconsin 34567

Dear Ms. Boone:

If you will grant me 30 minutes of your time I believe I can demonstrate that my unusual background of education and experience can be put to work immediately to the benefit of your corporate communications program at Olympiad Aircraft Corporation.

As you will see from the enclosed copy of an overview of my qualifications,* I will be graduating from the University of Warren in Oakville, Illinois this June. During my four years at the university, I have been fortunate enough to earn my degree and gain hands-on working experience that bears directly on a career in corporate communications and management. I have also gained valuable leadership experience in our profession and in the broader affairs of the student body.

I would appreciate any opportunity to discuss your needs and my qualifications. I will call your office on (date) for an appointment.

Sincerely yours,

Susan Powell

Note to the reader: You may choose to enclose your basic resume instead of the overview.

Example of letter as a follow-up to a job interview.

Mr. John Simpson
Vice President-Corporate Communications
Allied Manufacturing Company
123 Main Street
Moline, Illinois 12134

Dear Mr. Simpson:

Thank you for the time we spent together yesterday discussing my qualifications and how they might be put to work to help you advance Allied Manufacturing Company's corporate communications program.

I am particularly excited by the prospect of being involved with your community relations programs in the two areas where the company will be constructing new manufacturing facilities. I am confident that my education and working experience – particularly in media relations – would enable me to make a strong contribution to your efforts.

As we discussed, I am providing you with (1) the names of three persons you may contact as references; and (2) several more examples of my writing.

I believe that Allied Manufacturing and I would benefit by my joining your corporate communications staff. I look forward to further discussions with you and your staff.

Sincerely yours,

Susan Powell

Example of letter as a follow-up to a job interview.

Ms. Jane Campbell
Executive Secretary – Corporate Communications
Allied Manufacturing Company
123 Main Street
Moline, Illinois 12134

Dear Ms. Campbell:

I want to express my appreciation for all of your assistance as I was preparing for my interview with Mr. Simpson.

The information you provided about the company's activities and policies in its several plant communities was extremely helpful. The copies of the annual report and the chairman's speech to the State Chamber of Commerce provided me with important insights.

I feel that I had a positive interview yesterday with Mr. Simpson. He outlined some exciting projects to which I believe I could make a meaningful contribution based on my education and experience. I am very enthusiastic about the prospect of joining your organization.

Again, many thanks for your help. I look forward to seeing you again soon.

Sincerely yours,

Susan Powell

Example of letter accepting an offer of employment.

Mr. John Simpson
Vice President-Corporate Communications
Allied Manufacturing Company
123 Main Street
Moline, Illinois 12134

Dear Mr. Simpson:

I am proud and delighted to accept your offer of a position as Community Relations Representative in Allied Manufacturing's Corporate Communications Department.

The arrangements for my beginning employment on July 15, as outlined in your letter of July 1, are entirely satisfactory. Prior to that time I will have taken the medical examination in the company's health services offices and completed the various items of paperwork as required. In the meantime, I would appreciate receiving any additional information about the company, the upcoming expansion or the position I will be filling that would help me in preparing to begin my job.

I look forward with enthusiasm to joining your organization. I am convinced that both Allied Manufacturing and I will realize great benefits from this association.

Sincerely yours,

Susan Powell

Example of letter declining offer.

Ms. Mary Coleman
Vice President-Public Relations
Downing Computers, Inc.
678 Cedar Street
Royal, Illinois 98734

Dear Ms. Coleman:

Your offer of a position in Downing Computers' public relations department is greatly appreciated. I consider it a distinct honor to have been selected from among the many candidates for this position with your organization.

As I am sure you can appreciate, it has been a difficult decision for me. However, after weighing all the considerations, I have decided to accept a position as Community Relations Representative with Allied Manufacturing. I begin my employment with this fine company on July 15.

Please extend my appreciation and best wishes to those several members of your staff who were so courteous and helpful to me during the interviewing process.

I hope our paths cross often in the future. In the meantime, I wish you continued success with your excellent public relations programs that benefit both Downing Computers and those the company serves.

Sincerely yours,

Susan Powell

Example of letter acknowledging rejection of application.

Mr. James Humes
Vice President – Marketing
Scott Chemical Company
Jefferson Business Center
Oxford, Illinois 45678

Dear Mr. Humes:

As I am sure you will appreciate, I am disappointed that I was not chosen to fill the position of sales trainee with Scott Chemical Company. Yours is an outstanding company to which I believe I could have made a meaningful contribution.

However, I am aware there was strong competition for the position. I also understand that in the final analysis you chose someone with an education in chemical engineering.

There are several attractive prospects in my continuing search for a position in marketing. I am confident that one or more of these opportunities will materialize. In the meantime, I would appreciate your keeping the information about my qualifications in your file of active prospects.

Thank you again for your consideration of my qualifications.

Sincerely yours,

Thomas Chase

Example of letter announcing acceptance of job offer and expressing appreciation for assistance.

Ms. Judith Hailey
President
First Service Bank
678 Excel Avenue
Homestead, Illinois 67345

Dear Ms. Hailey:

I want to share my good news with you and thank you for your helping to make it happen.

I have accepted a position with Allied Manufacturing Company. My employment with this outstanding company begins July 15, when I assume a position as Community Relations Representative at the corporate headquarters in Moline.

I am particularly pleased that my first assignments will have to do with the company's opening of two new manufacturing facilities in central Illinois.

My search for employment would not have come to such a satisfactory conclusion without your help. I deeply appreciate the time you took to share with me your insights as to the ingredients required for a successful career. Your suggestions for contacts I should make proved to be invaluable.

I am indebted to you for your advice, support and confidence.

Sincerely yours,

Susan Powell

SPECIAL OFFER

A special JOB SEARCH CONTROL work kit is available from the publisher. This kit contains multiple copies of numerous forms and worksheets designed to help you organize and expedite your job search to a successful conclusion.

****

Multiple copies of HOW TO LAND YOUR FIRST JOB & MAKE A SUCCESS OF IT are available at discounted prices when purchased for educational, business or sales promotion purposes.

*****

For Information Contact
COMMON SENSE PUBLISHING COMPANY
P.O. Box 1581
Pine Bluff, Arkansas 71613
Telephone (501) 536-5468
Fax (501) 536-3344